The Harvard Business School Guide to Careers in the Nonprofit Sector

Stephanie Lowell
Harvard Business School, Class of 1999

IN ASSOCIATION WITH THE HARVARD BUSINESS SCHOOL SOCIAL ENTERPRISE CLUB AND THE INITIATIVE ON SOCIAL ENTERPRISE

ISBN 1-57851-231-X

Library of Congress Cataloging-in-Publication Data

Lowell, Stephanie, 1971–
    The Harvard Business School guide to careers in the nonprofit sector / Stephanie Lowell.
        p.   cm.
    ISBN 1-57851-231-X
    1. Nonprofit organizations—Vocational guidance—United States. 2. Associations,
institutions, etc.—Vocational guidance—United States. 3. Nonprofit organizations—United
States—Employees. 4. Associations, institutions, etc.—United States—Employees. I. Harvard University.
Harvard Business School.

HD2769.2.U6 L68 2000
331.7'02'0973—dc21
                                                                        99-049572

Contents

Foreword

Nonprofit organizations and other social enterprises play a critical role in addressing society's most pressing challenges. These organizations also represent a growing sector of the economy, one that is increasingly interrelated with the private sector. This growth has led to an expanding demand among nonprofit organizations for management skills and a corresponding desire among business leaders and corporations for an effective way to have a positive impact on the social sector.

Harvard Business School has become the setting for some remarkable activity focused on social enterprise. These efforts build on growing interest in nonprofits by our faculty, our students, and our alumni and reflect our view that social sector involvement is an integral component of business leadership.

The school launched the Initiative on Social Enterprise in 1993 with the support of John Whitehead, the vision of former Dean John McArthur, and the ongoing commitment of current Dean Kim Clark. Professors Jim Austin and Kash Rangan have provided outstanding leadership as founding co-chairs of the Initiative, and over forty faculty members from all areas of HBS have helped us embark on an ambitious agenda of MBA classroom activity,

executive programs, fieldwork, and practice-based research in the field of social enterprise.

At the student level, the Social Enterprise Club, as well as other related extracurricular efforts at HBS, has grown from a handful of involved students to hundreds of MBAs, further demonstrating the importance of social enterprise to our leaders of tomorrow.

This career guide offers invaluable practical advice to MBA students and graduates interested in social enterprise career opportunities and provides examples of the growing involvement of MBAs in the social sector. I believe that this book can help both current students and alumni make a difference in the world as leaders in nonprofit and social enterprise organizations.

I wish all of you the best as you consider taking the next step along your career path, while at the same time making a tremendous impact on this critical sector of the economy.

STEVEN R. NELSON
(Harvard Business School, MBA 1988)
Executive Director, Harvard Business School Initiative on
Social Enterprise

Message from John C. Whitehead

It gives me great pleasure to see how many MBAs are interested in the not-for-profit field. You have an important role to play in this sector as both business and community leaders. I believe that this career guide is an important resource that will help chart your course in the years ahead.

The not-for-profit sector is growing in importance both economically and socially. Not-for-profits account for over 10 percent of the United States workforce and 7 percent of the gross national product. These organizations are taking over many functions formerly managed by the government; at the same time, they face new forms of cooperation with—and competition from—for-profit business.

Running a not-for-profit is definitely more difficult than running a for-profit company. The challenges of not-for-profit management include finding creative ways to raise operational capital, motivating a diverse workforce without substantial financial incentives (including large pools of volunteers), and establishing meaningful tools to measure performance in the absence of profitability measures. On the other hand, this means that it can be much more satisfying to apply your business skills to not-for-profit endeavors. The impact you will have in the sector is hard to beat.

The Initiative on Social Enterprise is a major effort at Harvard Business School to address the growing importance of not-for-profit organizations and other private social-purpose enterprises. I am excited by the school's recent progress in developing community leaders as well as corporate leaders, and in integrating social enterprise in all aspects of the school: admissions, research and course development, job placement, and alumni activities.

As I think about my own career, I can tell you that the time I devote to not-for-profit organizations is incredibly rewarding. My dream is that more and more MBAs will become full-time not-for-profit senior managers, bringing to these organizations the same management talent available in the corporate sector.

I strongly encourage you to consider a career in the not-for-profit sector. As this career guide reveals, many challenging and rewarding opportunities lie ahead.

JOHN C. WHITEHEAD
(Harvard Business School, MBA 1947)
Chair, Harvard Business School Initiative on
Social Enterprise Advisory Board
Former Co-chairman, Goldman, Sachs & Company
Former United States Deputy Secretary of State

Preface

The majority of MBAs will leave school and enter the private sector—consulting, banking, high-tech start-ups, brand management, strategic planning . . . you know the list. The money is good, the prestige is high, and the path is fairly clear.

So why think about a nonprofit or social sector career? The applicability of your MBA skills to this sector is much more clear than it was ten years ago. In fact, top-quality management skills are among the most talked-about needs of nonprofit organizations. In the social sector, you can apply your hard-earned MBA skills to personally meaningful endeavors. The impact you will have on the community and the rewards of working in the field are tremendous. Furthermore, the levels of responsibility you will have from very early on in your career are hard to match in the corporate world. The words of a Harvard Business School alumna may convince you about the opportunities: "I love what I do. I run my own business, I'm continually challenged to think analytically and creatively, and I am surrounded by smart and talented people. I get to help women start their own businesses. I can't imagine doing anything else." (Andrea Silbert, Founder and Executive Director, Center for Women & Enterprise)

The idea for this career guide came about in response to the growing number of MBA students and alumni who have expressed both an interest in nonprofit management and a sense of frustration with the job-search process in the field. The recruiting process is not as formal as in the for-profit sector, and the career path is less clearly defined than more traditional "business" pursuits.

In the process of writing this book I heard concerns similar to the following:

- I know I want to work in education, but I have no idea how to start my job search.

- There are great resources available to help me find a consulting or banking job—but how do I find a position in a nonprofit organization?

- If I call up a nonprofit organization, I feel like they'll ask me to volunteer, but they won't know how to use my MBA skills.

- I would like to work for a nonprofit, but I need to pay off my business school loans.

- I don't want to get stuck in bureaucracy, but I want to have impact on social issues.

- I'm ready to make a career change and I think I want to work for a nonprofit—so how do I get started?

This guide will answer those questions and more.

Many people contributed significant time and energy to this effort. I would like to give very special thank-yous to Steve Nelson, Margot Keiper, and Bob Burakoff, who supported the project from its inception in innumerable ways, and to John Whitehead for his ongoing support of so many HBS Social Enterprise activities. I would also like to thank the HBS Social Enterprise Club and the club's Alumni Advisory Board members for their help throughout the process. Several other individuals deserve a show of appreciation for their input and support, including Bob Gardella, Pat Brandes, and Rosabeth Moss Kanter.

Several individuals contributed to this effort through interviewing, writing, and editing help, and deserve mention by name: Sarah Alexander, Jennifer Armini, Julie Barker, Lisa Baumgarten, Ben Besley, Jill Clark Hawley, Jon Cowan, Rebecca Davis, Ben Fenton, Kevin Glasgow, Meredith Bradley Jenkins, Karen Kaufman, Purnima Kochikar, Kathy Korman, Emily Lawson, Catherine Lovejoy, Shivam Mallick, Tori Pesek, Michelle Renbaum, David Stolow, Emily Sullivan, Sarah Thorp, Wendy Vanasselt, and Joshua Wallack. Special thanks to Michael Everett-Lane for his contribution as well as his sharp editing eye.

To the alumni and other interviewees, who graciously found the time to share their stories and to offer support and encouragement for the project: thank you, and keep up the great work!

And finally, to my family and friends, who read drafts of the guide whether or not they were interested in the subject, this book would not be here today without your help. Mom, Dad, Lisa, and Gregg, you made this possible. Thanks!

Introduction

You may want to read this book from cover to cover, or you may be looking for something specific and want to flip right to it. So here's a quick guide to the book itself.

1. Background on Social Enterprise and the Nonprofit Sector. This section defines and describes the various pieces of the broad field of social enterprise: private, nonprofit organizations; public sector organizations; social-purpose businesses; and socially responsible businesses. It sets the context for the rest of the book.

2. The Career Continuum. This section contains information on everything from summer internships, to mid-career job changes, to "retirement careers" and offers advice in the job search at all phases of your career. It also includes a discussion of the pros and cons of working for nonprofits at various stages of the continuum and provides information about volunteering and board membership, which are helpful steps along the way to your nonprofit career.

3. The Job-search Process. This section walks you through the steps of the nonprofit job search, which can differ significantly from the typical MBA recruiting process. It includes information on conducting background research, creating a hit list, doing informational interviews, contacting organizations, interviewing and following-up with your interviewer, and evaluating opportunities. It also discusses salary considerations and sources of financial support.

4. Managing Expectations. The nonprofit world differs from that of the for-profit, and this section describes key positions in nonprofit organizations, cultural differences, pros and cons of working in the sector, and some myths and misconceptions about nonprofit careers.

5. Subsector Overviews. The book contains overviews of twelve nonprofit subsectors: arts and culture, community economic development, community development financial institutions, education, environment, foundations, government, health care, international aid and economic development, social services, social purpose businesses, and socially responsible business/corporate community relations. Each contains an overview of the area and any subdivisions (for example, housing development as a subdivision of community economic development), hot topics in the field, and roles for MBAs.

6. Resource Road Map. The road map begins with a list of general resources on the nonprofit sector and career-related publications and organizations. It then lists organizations and resources by subsector, with additional sections about volunteering and board membership. The organization lists in this road map are by no means exhaustive—organizations were chosen because they are known to be well-run, fairly large (with some exceptions), and receptive to working with MBAs.

7. Nonprofit Profiles. Profiles of Harvard Business School alumni in nonprofit careers are interspersed throughout the book. Their stories give a sense of what it is like to work in the field the person has chosen, as well as a look at the process they went through to get there, which may give you some ideas for your own job search. The profiles are integrated into relevant sections. For example, while you are reading about foundations you will find the story of Kim Lew (Harvard Business School, MBA 1992), a portfolio strategist at the Ford Foundation in New York.

CHAPTER ONE

Background on Social Enterprise and the Nonprofit Sector

Overview

Broadly defined, social enterprise includes nonprofit organizations, public-sector/government entities, and (for-profit) social-purpose businesses. Stanford Professor Greg Dees has developed a framework called the Social Enterprise Spectrum, which describes a continuum from purely philanthropic nonprofit organizations to purely commercial for-profit organizations, with a variety of hybrids in between.[1] Though a social enterprise organization can take a variety of legal/organizational forms, each entity along the social enterprise spectrum has public and/or social issues as an integral part of its mission.

Private, Nonprofit Organizations

On the broadest level, the nonprofit sector (otherwise known as the independent sector, the social sector, and the not-for-profit sector) includes organizations in the United States that focus on social issues and are neither government nor traditional businesses. Academically speaking, nonprofits share at least five key characteristics: they (1) are organizations; (2) are not part of the government; (3) do not distribute profits to shareholders; (4) are self-governing; and (5) serve some public purpose.[2]

The nonprofit sector includes nearly 1.5 million organizations in the United States alone, spending nearly $500 billion each year. About 6 percent of all U.S. organizations are nonprofit, and one in fifteen Americans works for a nonprofit (a total of over 7 percent of the paid labor force).[3] In other countries nonprofits are often called NGOs (for nongovernmental organizations) and play similar societal roles. Although the United States has the world's largest nonprofit sector, many developed and developing nations have seen strong growth in their own nonprofit activity. For more information on international nonprofit organizations, see Lester Salamon and Helmut Anheir's book, which reports the results of a large Johns Hopkins University project comparing nonprofit activity in six developed and five developing countries.

Nonprofit organizations can be further segmented into those that are member-serving (for example, labor unions, political parties, professional associations) and those that are public-serving (religious, charitable, or social welfare institutions). Member-serving organizations are tax exempt, but donations to them are not tax deductible. The public-serving organizations are the ones that we most often think of as nonprofits, and that qualify as 501(c)(3) and 501(c)(4) organizations (tax designations primarily indicative of tax deductibility of donations).

Nonprofits can be categorized by the role they play as well as by the issues they address. By role, nonprofits fall into four major categories: service providers (such as homeless shelters, schools); support providers (such as a technical assistance nonprofit that helps train others); funders (such as foundations); and advocacy organizations (such as the NAACP). Nonprofit organizations address an incredibly wide range of issues, including education, health, environment, civil rights, social services, and others. We address these categories in the second half of the guide through the subsector overviews. Note that these categorizations are meant to help you think through the role you might play in social enterprise rather than to create a theoretical (and academically pure) industry framework.

Public Organizations

The government is involved in nearly every aspect of social enterprise. Individuals and organizations in the public sector create public policy, allocate funds to social enterprise programs, regulate the sector, and provide services. They are involved with every subsector of the nonprofit world (and beyond), from education (for example, public schools), to health (the Department of Public Health), to environment (the EPA), to child care (such as Head Start), to arts and culture (such as the NEA), to public transportation and defense. And of course, the government operates at the national, state, and local levels and through elected, appointed, and hired (civil service) positions.

The section on the government/public sector will shed more light on how to pursue careers in this area by profiling MBAs who have made their mark through a variety of roles in the public sector.

Social Purpose Businesses

Simply stated, social purpose businesses are for-profit entities created to achieve a social or public-serving mission. For example, Community Wealth Ventures (CWV) designs and builds "community wealth enterprises" by providing consulting and technical assistance to non-profits, foundations, and corporate clients (see profile of Sarah Perry, chapter 5). CWV is actually a for-profit subsidiary of the nonprofit organization Share Our Strength, a national hunger relief organization.

Related Concepts

"Socially responsible business" is a common buzzword referring to businesses that try to balance the bottom line with a sense of social mission, or to do good while doing well. They also adopt "socially responsible" policies, addressing a broad range of issues from child care and family-friendly workplaces to environmental concerns, human rights, and corporate-community partnerships. For example, the goal of Stonyfield Farm, a yogurt producer, is to "produce the best-tasting, healthiest yogurt possible and to try to do some good in the world along the 'whey.'" The company promotes consumer awareness and participation in local and global environmental issues on its packaging, and donates 10 percent of profits to restore the environment. At Timberland, a sense of social responsibility, driven by the CEO's commitment to community issues, pervades the organization. The company's deep relationship with City Year is testament to its involvement in the community (see Harvard Business School Case 9-796-156).

Business leaders have become increasingly aware that their business performance is linked to the strength of the communities in which they operate, and that they have a role to play in the community as well as in the corporation. Harvard Business School Professor Rosabeth Moss Kanter comments, "It is increasingly clear that the next step in transforming American corporations is to transform the relationship between business and society."

Traditionally, corporate-community involvement has been limited to financial donations. But companies have begun to take a more innovative approach to the social sector, as highlighted in a 1998 HBS conference chaired by Professor Kanter, entitled "Business Leadership in the Social Sector." The conference highlighted initiatives such as Bell Atlantic's Project Explore—which used the Union City, New Jersey, public schools as a beta site for new technology, while using the new technology to enhance the educational experience for public school students. Such win-win business-community partnerships are becoming more common. Working in the community relations department of a large company is one way to get involved in such business-community projects from the corporate side (see profile of Nancy Lane, chapter 5).

Though socially responsible businesses (and corporate-community relations specifically) are viable forums for addressing social enterprise issues through the corporate sector, they are not social enterprise organizations per se. And though the subsector sections and the Resource Road Map in this book will provide some more information about these topics, the bulk of the guide will focus on careers in the nonprofit sector.

Overlaps and Partnerships

Despite clear definitional distinctions among the various sectors, partnerships have become increasingly common and increasingly important. Business, government, and nonprofit organizations are interdependent and can benefit greatly from cooperation with one another. Significant emphasis has been placed in recent years on the concept of public-private and corporate-nonprofit partnerships.

Notes

1. Greg Dees, "Enterprising Nonprofits." *Harvard Business Review,* January–February 1998: 54–67.

2. Lester Salamon and Helmut Anheir, *The Emerging Nonprofit Sector: An Overview* (Manchester: Manchester University Press, 1996).

3. National Center for Nonprofit Boards (www.ncnb.org).

JOHN SAWHILL

Business, government, and nonprofit leadership

"I have the best job in America," says John Sawhill, CEO and president of The Nature Conservancy (TNC). "I work with talented, interesting, committed people. I really feel like I'm doing something important for society and for future generations. And I get to see some of the most interesting places in the world, such as the beautiful rain forests of Papua New Guinea."

Sawhill leads The Nature Conservancy's worldwide environmental preservation efforts and is involved with a number of boards in both the for-profit and nonprofit sectors. But he is also a prime example of someone who has made several intersector transitions, from corporate, to government, to nonprofit leadership positions.

As a newly minted Princeton graduate in 1958, Sawhill entered Merrill Lynch's Junior Executive Training Program. Since he had no business background from his college years, Sawhill decided to take some courses at New York University (NYU), and "ended up" completing a Ph.D. in economics and becoming an assistant dean at the university. Still, he thought he wanted to be in business, and he found a job with Commercial Credit in Baltimore, a company focused on sales and finance. After a few years, an opportunity arose to work with McKinsey & Company, Inc., and Sawhill took it, only to return to Commercial Credit a few years later to run the Business Services Group (overseeing all commercial leasing) when the company experienced a major change in senior management.

"Then one day my assistant said, 'John, the White House is on the phone.'" This was in 1968, the early days of the Nixon Administration, and Nixon was looking for an associate director of energy, science, and natural resources (one of four major positions under the budget director). Sawhill was excited by the opportunity, but "I had to tell them I was a registered Democrat." Nixon accepted that fact, and Sawhill became a government official. Soon after his appointment, "the oil embargo and the energy crisis hit. The President cre-

ated the Federal Energy Administration, and I was made deputy director under Bill Simon, and then director when Bill became the Treasury secretary. Those days were crazy. We had sixty days to hire 4,000 people and to create regulations for the whole U.S. oil industry."

Sawhill stayed in the federal government when Ford became President, "until I went on the *Today Show* and said that the government should raise the gas tax. Then Ford fired me." So Sawhill made his way back to NYU, which at the time was in need of a new president. "It was great timing," says Sawhill. "And at the time I was fairly visible. I had had a lot of publicity through my government work—on TV, testifying before Congress, etc." Sawhill became president of NYU, where his McKinsey experience helped him address the university's fairly significant management problems and need of financial restructuring.

Five years later, the White House called again. This time it was President Carter, who asked Sawhill to be his deputy secretary of energy. "What could I say other than 'yes, Mr. President'?" So Sawhill returned to Washington. When Carter left office, Sawhill did too—and returned to McKinsey as a director in the Washington, D.C., office. Sawhill led the development of McKinsey's energy practice until 1989 when he left McKinsey once again, this time for his current position as CEO of The Nature Conservancy.

Sawhill has always sought out organizations "where I'm learning all the time," and has found that each sector provides different learning challenges. "At McKinsey the major challenges are how to solve problems, to think creatively about solutions, and to work effectively with teams. In government, you have to understand how to work in a very complicated, interrelated environment, where you have to talk with X before Y, but after Z, to get things accomplished. In nonprofit organizations, where people are generally values-driven, you have to lead differently than you would in the corporate

> *"What could I say other than 'yes, Mr. President'?"*

sector, and it's a more participative decision-making process." Sawhill notes that the skills he learned in each environment helped him manage more effectively in the others.

The Nature Conservancy is an international, private, nonprofit conservation organization committed to the preservation of ecologically significant land and the diversity of life it supports. To date the organization and its members have been responsible for the protection of more than nine million acres of ecologically significant land. TNC is a very "business-oriented" nonprofit. "We buy, swap, and trade land and are engaged in constant negotiation," says Sawhill. "We love to do complex transactions." TNC is also very decentralized. Since land is managed locally, TNC staff need to be part of the community to affect the way the community thinks about the land and the need for preservation. Thus Sawhill's role is "to set and communicate the direction and values that will help everyone make decisions in their area." TNC is run by what Sawhill terms "loose-tight management": clear, centralized mission and values to drive individual autonomy and decision making.

Though Sawhill enjoyed his years in business and in government, "I think if I had to do it all over I would go to the nonprofit sector sooner. TNC has been my most challenging and rewarding experience." To current MBAs he gives this advice: "It's important to decide what turns you on, and then to do something that enables you to work in that area. You can get into a position of leadership and responsibility much earlier in a nonprofit, in part because of less competition." But most importantly, Sawhill believes that a learning environment is the best place to be: "Constant learning keeps you interested, alive, and excited."

CHAPTER TWO

The Career Continuum

Overview

Before you get started on your job search, you need to step back and think about your long-term career aspirations. Where have you been? Where would you like to be next year, five years from now, after retirement? At each stage of the career continuum different considerations will influence your job-search strategy.

Before going forward, write down a few things about your career goals, including:

- Experiences you've had and skills you've developed before, during, or after business school

- Long-term goals

- Goals for the job you're seeking right now

- Subject (e.g., child care) and functional (e.g., marketing) interests

- Organizational characteristics you like and dislike (e.g., size, location)

- What you really care about . . . and what you enjoy doing enough to do it every day

Now, think about the career continuum from summer internship to your job five or ten years out, to retirement from the working world. Where are you now? How does the career decision you are about to make fit into your long-term goals? Decisions made and skills developed at each stage will shape the direction of your ultimate career path. The next several minisections of the guide address the various decision points and critical job/career considerations at each point of the career continuum.

Summer Internship

The summer internship is a fairly low-risk job experience that will prepare you for the post-MBA job decision. This is a good time to experiment in a field you know little about, or to get a stronger sense of what it means to work in a specific area or a specific organization in which you already have an interest.

When contemplating summer internship possibilities, ask yourself the following questions:

- What is your longer-term career goal? How does this summer job fit in with that goal?

- Are you looking for a high level of responsibility by working in a nonprofit to distinguish yourself from others when you reenter the private sector after graduation?

- Do you want experience in the nonprofit sector—or in a specific organization—over the summer to set the stage for a longer-term nonprofit career?

- Do you want for-profit experience (especially if you've come from a nonprofit background) to reinforce the business skills that you can bring to the nonprofit sector after graduation?

- What experience did you have prior to school? How will this summer job strengthen skills or fill in skill/experience gaps? Which aspect is more important to you?

- Is there something you think you may be interested in, but aren't sure? This is a great time to experiment and to try something "out of the box."

Just as many MBAs use a summer associate position with a consulting firm or investment bank as an entrée into a full-time job opportunity after graduation, social enterprise summer internships can lead to full-time offers. Mike Sweeney (Harvard Business School, MBA 1998) spent the summer of 1997 working on The Nature Conservancy's strategic vision in the field of conservation and developing a proposal for a Conservation Learning Network, and then joined The Nature Conservancy full-time after graduation. His classmate, Lisa Schorr, profiled in this chapter, found that her summer work with the Pine Street Inn led to her current position as director of business enterprise development with the organization. On the other hand, many MBAs who have come from nonprofit or public sector backgrounds use the summer to experience what it's like to work in a private sector organization and to reinforce their business school skills in that setting. The profile of Jennifer Brown Simon (Harvard Business School, MBA 1994) later in this chapter illustrates that path well.

LISA SCHORR

From summer position to a full-time job

For Lisa Schorr (Harvard Business School, MBA 1998), the Community Enterprise Summer Fellow position was a great experience in and of itself, as well as an entrée to a long-term relationship with the Pine Street Inn.

Community Enterprise is a partnership between HBS and McKinsey & Company's Boston office that provides consulting teams to Boston-area community organizations for twelve weeks to address major strategic issues. "That summer was fantastic. It gave me the opportunity to do exactly what I wanted to do when I came to business school: bring business and management skills to social-service organizations. And the program provided strong supervision and support to help me do it."

Schorr came to business school after four years at City Year in Boston. "I had volunteered with City Year on and off through college, and knew I wanted to work there full-time when I graduated." She spent her first year as a corps member working in an elementary school, her second as a special assistant to the City Year co-director, her third as a team leader, and her fourth in charge of service activities in Boston. Schorr loved all four years. She was able to explore a wide variety of social-service activities and work with a diverse group of people, and had the chance to work with corporate and community leaders around the country. "I had tremendous responsibility from very early on, and many opportunities for leadership."

But after four years, Schorr began to feel slightly frustrated. Though she was impressed with the City Year management's talent and innovation, she felt that additional business skills would enhance the organization's ability to achieve its mission. With that in mind, she de-

"The nonprofit job search at business school is harder and lonelier than the typical path to consulting or brand management."

cided to apply to business school to learn about management and "bring it back to the nonprofit sector."

During the summer of 1997, Schorr and classmate Kirsten Steward (Harvard Business School, MBA 1998) consulted to the Pine Street Inn (PSI) through the Community Enterprise Program. Pine Street—New England's largest homeless shelter—wanted to develop new business ventures that would help Inn residents develop basic job skills, through a full-time job outside the shelter, as an interim step between long-term unemployment and self-sufficiency. They also wanted these ventures to be at least self-sustaining if not income-generating. PSI had generated many new business ideas but needed a way to evaluate the opportunities. With support from a McKinsey engagement manager and from Bob Burakoff, director of the Community Enterprise Program, Schorr and Steward developed a template and evaluation process. They narrowed the field of ideas to two near-term opportunities—expansion of the used-clothing operation and a new contract packaging business—and wrote a business plan for each. In the end, they chose to focus on the clothing business as the first major opportunity to pursue.

Schorr, Steward, and two more classmates continued to work with PSI through a second-year field-study project. They worked on implementation and developed a longer-term strategy to achieve PSI's goal of developing a portfolio of businesses and employment opportunities. The team recommended that PSI hire someone to work on the project full-time by February. But by May the organization still had not hired anyone because they had been waiting for special grant funding from the Boston Foundation to support the position. Pine Street considered a number of candidates and narrowed the field to two—Schorr and one other. The other candidate had "a lot more experience in new business development, but no nonprofit experience."

Schorr believes that her history of nonprofit work, including front-line work at City Year and strategic work at PSI while in business school, combined with the basic business capabilities and credibility she had from the MBA, won her the position. From Schorr's perspective, the fit was great. Though she had identified other exciting opportunities, the job at Pine Street seemed too good to turn down. "It's a very unique organization. It has an institutional side that manages to efficiently and effectively serve huge groups of homeless people everyday, nonstop. Yet there are also pockets of innovation throughout the organization, which is a very rare combination in nonprofit or for-profit companies."

Schorr has been very pleased with her role as director of business enterprise development, which includes a wide range of responsibilities. She supervises the current Pine Street portfolio businesses, looks for new opportunities, evaluates them, and thinks about how to finance new start-ups. She works with other organizations and manages public communications about Pine Street's new business enterprises, and is in the process of developing an advisory board. And she is on the senior management team, "so I get to apply my business school learning to general management of the organization in addition to doing business enterprise development work."

Relationships developed through summer internships, field studies, and volunteer consulting projects can be extremely helpful in a future job search. "The nonprofit job search at business school is harder and lonelier than the typical path to consulting or brand management. I benefited a lot from my past experience and connections after several years in Boston. And the Community Enterprise experience certainly helped a tremendous amount," says Schorr. "I don't know how people get into the sector if they've never experienced it before, at least through some aspect of volunteering."

JENNIFER BROWN SIMON

Summer for-profit experience

"When I arrived at the Washington Tennis Foundation two years ago, the place was in shambles. The previous executive director was a great visionary, but the organization lacked sound management. It had $1,000 in the bank and was hundreds of thousands of dollars in debt. My challenge was to turn it around—in terms of finances, strategy, and overall morale. So I started piece by piece—taking each aspect of the organization, examining it, and then creating a strategic plan. My HBS and McKinsey experiences helped me sort through the problems, communicate my thoughts well, and teach others to do the same."

"I'm happier than probably anyone I know because I truly love what I do."

As of 1999, the Washington Tennis Foundation—under Executive Director Jennifer Brown Simon (Harvard Business School, MBA 1994)—had no debt, $300,000 in the bank, and an annual budget twice that of when she arrived. "It's amazing how much impact basic business skills had on this organization. Even tools such as financial spreadsheets on Excel were new to them and had huge impact on the organization right away. Plus, I think that funders were more confident that their money would be well-used because there was a business person at the helm of the organization. But I had to make some very tough business decisions in an environment that was not used to such a mind-frame, including firing some long-term poor performers and outsourcing some previously internal functions. This is particularly difficult when you are an outsider, a 'business person,' moving in, but it's something that had to be done. Once things were financially stable, and once people were confident that we had a solid strategic plan, the organization really took off. There was a positive ripple effect throughout the staff and the board, and into the community."

Brown Simon's preMBA experience was primarily public sector-focused. "I always knew I wanted to work in the community, and after college I went to work on Capitol Hill. But I felt distant from the people I wanted to help—political work was too policy-oriented, and hands-on work was more my style. So I applied to the Kennedy School of Government (KSG), thinking that I would learn more about policy and nonprofit management to potentially run a grassroots organization. During my first year I lived in Soldiers Field Park (located on the HBS campus), and as I heard business school students talk about their courses, I realized that learning management at HBS could be really important for me." She applied to HBS, was accepted, and decided to do a joint HBS/KSG program.

Brown Simon had spent the summer before HBS (and after the first year of KSG) in East Africa, working with the International Rescue Committee on a food distribution system to respond to a regional drought. "So you can imagine the culture shock when I returned and began the first year of business school. I really had no business background, and I felt somewhat out of place at first. But I gradually settled into the routine, and when interview season began I thought, 'what the heck,' and applied to consulting firms with everyone else. It seemed like a great way to apply the skills I was learning, and I did feel that I needed some private sector experience." Brown Simon decided to spend the summer at McKinsey.

After business school, Brown Simon returned to McKinsey for two years. "I knew that the skills I would further develop there would be a real asset, but I also knew that I would miss direct community involvement and impact. So I set in my mind that I would stay for two years and no more, which is what I did. I'm definitely happy that I spent time at McKinsey. It sharpened my skills beyond the theoretical learning of business school, it gave me credibility, and it broadened my perspective on many issues." Once she left McKinsey, Brown Simon embarked on a two-month intensive job search. "I knew I wanted to work in a direct-service organization, and I knew I wanted to work with inner-city kids. A director at McKinsey was very helpful—sending out letters and helping me make contacts for infor-

mational interviews. One of his contacts was on the board of the Washington Tennis Foundation, and she let me know that they were looking for an executive director."

The Washington Tennis Foundation runs after-school, weekend, and summer programs for primarily inner-city children, starting in second grade. "Actually, we're changing the name to the Washington Tennis and Education Foundation. We teach tennis, literacy, and life skills, both at our own facility and in the communities. We then take the children who are dedicated to the program and seem to have high potential, and put them in a more intensive program of tennis and college preparation." Having played competitive tennis as an undergraduate at Yale University, Brown Simon was extremely excited about the opportunity to run the organization. "It was much more of a risk for them than for me. Here I was, a young white woman with little real management experience, about to become the executive director of a diverse, inner-city organization." But everything has worked out well for both.

"My advice to MBAs is to be careful not to come on too strong. Because you have an MBA, you may be stereotyped as 'too business-like' or 'arrogant' or 'a cost-cutter.' You need to position your MBA as a toolbox, and let the staff and board know that you understand and respect the culture and want to use business skills to help it grow and become effective, not completely change it. You also have to realize that you can learn a tremendous amount from your staff, if you are open to seeing others' perspectives on issues. All of the general management cases touched on these personnel issues, but you learn on the job just how important people skills really are."

One drawback to jumping into the executive director role was that Brown Simon had no direct mentor from whom to learn the ropes. "It's hard when you don't have someone right above you to observe and learn from, but I have still learned a ton. I learn from my staff, I learn from the kids, I seek out other executive directors, and I work closely with selected members of the board whom I particularly respect."

And the best part of the job? "I go out to the classrooms and the courts as much as possible. Seeing the kids out there learning and so happy to be in the program is the best part. It's my reason for being here. I'm happier than probably anyone I know because I truly love what I do."

First Job after Business School

Most of today's MBA graduates will work for several different organizations over the course of their careers. So the first job decision is not a be-all or end-all. However, it is important, and the decision-making process can be stressful.

You may be struggling with the question of whether to go into nonprofit work right after graduation or to work in the for-profit sector for a few more years and enter the nonprofit arena later in your career. This is a common dilemma for MBAs, particularly those that worked in the private sector before business school. Based on interviews with students and alumni, Table 2-1 describes some of the pros and cons of each option.

Pat Brandes, chief operating officer of the United Way of Massachusetts Bay, comments "If you have a vision, or see a nonprofit organization with a vision that speaks to you, go directly after it. If not, find a job that gives you the greatest opportunity both to explore your passions and to build skills—whether that be in a for-profit or a nonprofit organization."

Neil Silverston (Harvard Business School, MBA 1987), president of WorkSource Staffing Partnership, adds, "There are two schools of thought: you can make money early on and get into social enterprise work when you have the flexibility, or you can go directly into it after graduation. I would encourage you to consider this: if you believe that you have the ability to change the world, go for it now!"

But, as one alumnus comments, "ultimately you have to decide for yourself . . . and make the decision based on what you feel in your gut. No one else can tell you what is right for you."

Many students cite financial considerations as a major obstacle to entering the nonprofit sector right out of business school. However, while your salary ceiling will be much lower than that of your professional-service firm peers, the nonprofit salary floors are not nearly as low as many might expect. "Nonprofits are beginning to recognize that they have to find the resources to pay for management skills, and taking a nonprofit job does not necessarily mean making a huge sacrifice," notes Schorr (profiled earlier in this chapter). While you won't start with a six-figure salary, an offer from $50,000 up to $70,000—especially in the larger nonprofit organizations—is not out of reach.

Still, the tradeoffs can be difficult. One alumna makes this comment about balancing financial considerations in

the career decision: "I came from a low-income background, and I knew that when I left business school I had no option but to take a job that paid enough for me to pay off my loans. It is always a hard decision to sacrifice a high salary, but when people rely on you financially it is even more difficult, if not impossible. So I temporarily deviated from my ultimate vision—to consult to urban economic development organizations—in order to fulfill my financial obligations."

Table 2-1

Trade-offs in Choosing a Nonprofit Job Right Out of School

Choice	Pros	Cons
Directly into nonprofit	• Move into area of high responsibility early; work with very senior-level people in the organization and on the board • Do what you love; have impact on the community • Develop community contacts	• May be harder to go from nonprofit to for-profit organizations in your later career *(but definitely not impossible)* • May miss out on some business management skill development opportunities • Lower salaries than most for-profit jobs.
Working for a for-profit company first	• Learn on practical level the strategic/business skills that are needed in nonprofits (e.g., marketing, finance)—and applying the theory you learn in cases to real-life situations • Earn more money/pay off loans • Establish contacts/network in business world (for later fund-raising and partnerships) • Possibly enter at higher level once you do make the transition to a nonprofit	• Why wait to go into social enterprise if you know it's what you want to do? • May signal less commitment to nonprofit community; may be harder to enter later on *(but definitely not impossible)* • Corporate culture can be stifling or offer less responsibility early on than nonprofit organizations do

TED PRESTON

Moving right in

"All I see is opportunity," says Ted Preston (Harvard Business School, MBA 1998) of his job as director of educational programming at The Community Builders Inc. (TCB), a nonprofit developer of affordable housing, focusing on the comprehensive revitalization of neighborhoods. "We're a growing organization, we have a well-defined strategy, and we're doing cutting-edge work. Plus, TCB gave me a solid platform from which to get involved in education—which is what I've always said I wanted to do. Really, what more could I ask from my first job out of business school?"

Before coming to business school, Preston had been both a high school teacher and the executive director of Summerbridge Cincinnati, a nonprofit organization that prepares middle school students for rigorous high school programs and provides apprenticeships in teaching for high school and college students. "At Summerbridge I spent as much time learning to run an organization as I did thinking about education itself. The experience piqued my interest in management and operations, which is what eventually brought me to business school."

"I took this job because I knew the responsibility and opportunity would be tremendous, and I haven't been disappointed at all."

"In the MBA program I learned how to structure problems effectively, to develop a viable business model, and to really understand the market shaping your business needs. Especially as nonprofits operate more like for-profits, the need to think about competitors, customers, and yes, even complementors is really important."

Preston always knew deep down that he wanted to pursue entrepreneurial opportunities in education. After spending the summer of 1997 at Monitor Company, a management consulting firm—where he "learned a ton but missed the direct involvement in education and operations"—he sat down and revisited his personal mission. "I reread my application essay, and there it was: 'I want to gain the management skills to build and run a school.'" The question that remained was how to pursue that path from where he was.

"What they say is true, that you're at business school to create a network, and when I got back after the summer I found a group of people through the HBS Social Enterprise Club that shared my interest and helped provide support in my job search. Club members Sarah Thorp, Josh Freeman, Dan Ennis, and I spent a lot of time together building the social enterprise network among current students and alumni." The club also connected Preston to his future employer. Preston met Swan Oey, TCB's finance director and a member of the club's alumni advisory board, at one of the advisory board meetings. "Swan and I started to talk, and we both got excited." Preston liked the organization's forward-thinking approach to community issues, and Oey saw a fit between Preston's background and interests and TCB's strategic direction.

"The hard part about pursuing nonprofit jobs is that you have to be a lot more proactive in the interview process. I met with Swan, and then it took a few months and several phone calls to get back in the door, even though he told me they were interested in me. When I finally got in and met with the executive director, we talked about what they were considering doing in the field of education. Rather than let the opportunity slip, I went home, wrote a ten-page strategy document on how to improve the K–12 system in TCB's existing communities given their skills and resources, and sent it to him right away. That document got me the job. He called me back and the rest is history."

At TCB, Preston is responsible for developing the organization's education strategy, managing specific projects to improve educational offerings in TCB communities, and working on a service management project in the property management division to improve maintenance quality in the more than 5,000 housing units it manages. "I took this job because I knew the responsibility and opportunity would be tremendous, and I haven't been disappointed at all."

Asked if he has any words of wisdom for current MBAs interested in nonprofit careers, Preston offers a few suggestions. "Look for nonprofits where there are other business-oriented managers around." The MBA curriculum helps develop management skills that are applicable in for-profit and nonprofit businesses alike. Targeting organizations where other MBAs already work can help you find entrepreneurial, business-like nonprofits where you can leverage those skills to make an impact on the social-sector problems to which you are drawn.

Five to Ten Years Out

Some alumni have found that after a few years in "big business" they start to question the meaning of their work, or miss working in the community. Others have always had a plan in mind to go into the nonprofit sector but decided to gain some business expertise and contacts in the for-profit sector first. Either way, making the transition three to five or even ten years out is a common experience.

A few things to think about if you are currently five to ten years out and ready to make the transition:

- The search will be a networked job search—have patience. If you know in advance that you want to move into social enterprise after a certain number of years, put out feelers and develop a network while you're in your private-sector job—don't try to make the transition all at once.

- You may take a pay cut, even with an increase in responsibility level. Make sure you have a sense of the tradeoffs you are and are not willing to make.

- Especially if you are trying to enter a more established nonprofit, specific skills such as marketing or finance will be extremely appealing. "You have to think about what skills you bring that we don't already have," notes Brandes of the United Way of Massachusetts Bay. "Marketing and finance are often good entry points, especially if you have no program expertise. And then over time you can expand your role beyond these functions."

- How should you position yourself? You will have to pitch both your business skills and your commitment to the cause. Discussing your volunteer or pro-bono involvement and how it relates to your ability to succeed in this new nonprofit position will be critical.

If you are currently an MBA student or in an early stage of your (nonsocial enterprise) career, but plan to make a transition later on, there are some things you should be thinking about now:

- What skills will you want to have under your belt when you do make the transition? How can you make sure that you are developing those capabilities?

- What are you doing in the pretransition period to make sure that you stay connected to the nonprofit world, so that the transition will be made easier at that point (such as volunteering, serving on boards, doing pro bono work, etc.)?

PATRICK AITCHESON

A mid-career switch

"It's hard to make the switch from business school and the for-profit world to nonprofits," says Patrick Aitcheson (Harvard Business School, MBA 1992), director of the Union Settlement Family Child Care Network in East Harlem. Yet Aitcheson's career path shows that such a mid-career switch is possible, with perseverance.

After graduating from the Massachusetts Institute of Technology, Aitcheson spent three years at Lee Capital Holdings, a leveraged buyout firm in Boston. "I went to business school to make the transition into operations," he says, and after graduation went to work for Formica Corporation. He worked as a plant controller in Cincinnati for two years and then went on to manage a solid surfacing manufacturing plant of 250 employees in eastern Pennsylvania. After two and a half years of running the plant, Aitcheson decided that his next career move would be to buy and run his own business. But before committing to a new venture, he decided to take a year off and travel in Australia. "I wanted to travel while I was young, and before I committed to running a business for the next five to eight years."

While he was traveling, Aitcheson's plans changed. "I realized during the trip that what I really liked about my job was working with the people on the plant floor. We had GED and literacy classes and leadership training. So I thought, why not go to a nonprofit where I can really focus on this work?" When he returned to the States, he was referred by a former classmate to the New York City Investment Fund (NYCIF), a $60-million "social investing fund" chaired by Henry Kravis that promotes job growth and business development in New York City. At the time, NYCIF was considering a deal with the United Neighborhood Houses (UNH), a network of community-based organizations in New York City, to create jobs and increase the supply of child care by creating a network of family child-care providers. (Family child-care providers are generally entrepreneurs who look after children in their own homes.) Aitcheson saw an opportunity: "I volunteered to write a business plan for a large-scale family child-care network. Writing the plan was a way to get to know the nonprofit world and make contacts."

One of UNH's member organizations, the Union Settlement Association, hired Aitcheson to spend six months on the start-up phase of its Family Child Care Network. "After six months, we were supposed to hire a full-time director. But after that time, I decided I wanted to apply for the job myself." Having demonstrated his abilities and commitment, Aitcheson was hired. He now runs a program that serves 175 children and plans to expand to 600 children within five years.

"Be down to earth, don't talk all the time about your MBA experience, and just be part of the team. I've seen MBAs really crash and burn by walking in and assuming they have all the answers."

Aitcheson's nine-month "apprenticeship" was an important learning experience. "It was a process of getting to know people and deciding whether this was an area and an organization I wanted to work in. At the same time, the nonprofit had a chance to get to know me, and to use me even though I didn't have any experience in child care." Aitchenson's time at the NYCIF and at Union Settlement helped demonstrate his commitment. "It's hard to get in at the operations level mid-career if you haven't done nonprofit work before. Typically, either people work their way up in the nonprofit world, or they retire after decades of corporate work and sit on boards. So people are wondering about you—who you are, and can you live in the nonprofit world, which is *very* different. It's a whole different approach than making widgets and selling them to someone." He definitely recommends doing volunteer work as a way to "get a feel for what's out there and network, just like you'd do in the for-profit world. It's easier to convince people you're serious. Nonprofits can't afford to pay a lot, and they can't afford to make a mistake. Since there are not many high-level management people in a nonprofit organization, you really need to sell yourself—and know what you're getting into."

Aitcheson has found that humility is an important part of the process of "fitting in" to the nonprofit environment. "Be down to earth, don't talk all the time about your MBA experience, and just be part of the team. I've seen MBAs really crash and burn by walking in and assuming they have all the answers. You've got to sell your ideas—especially to people who have been in the industry for decades."

Another important aspect of the transition was the nature of the nonprofit and the nature of the work. Aitcheson "was looking for the part of the nonprofit world that was entrepreneurial." The NYCIF, for instance, "is in-between nonprofit and for-profit." And while Union Settlement is a traditional community-based social-service agency serving 12,000 people a year, Aitcheson found that "Union Settlement's approach is also more entrepreneurial than a typical nonprofit. We're moving forward with our expansion, even though we don't have all the funding in place."

Like any entrepreneur in a start-up phase, Aitcheson does "everything," including creating an organizational structure, managing employees, fund-raising, marketing the program to clients, creating a training program, creating and providing ongoing support services to clients, and designing a database and information technology systems. "Down the road, as the program grows, I hope to be less involved in doing everything and more able to delegate a lot of this work to others."

It's a long way from the Formica plant in Pennsylvania to the streets of East Harlem, but at Union Settlement, Aitcheson has realized his goal of running his own business.

Later-Life Transition

The trend of managers leaving the corporate world after many years to join a nonprofit organization has been picking up over recent years. And like most later-life career transitions, a shift to the nonprofit sector will be a networked job search. The more people you know and talk with in the field—whether nonprofit managers or board members—the easier your search will be. As Andrew Falender (Harvard Business School, MBA 1971), executive director of the Appalachian Mountain Club (see profile in chapter 4), notes about his own career path, major transitions are often "a matter of timing and luck." This is true in the for-profit field as well.

Seeking out others who have made similar career switches is one very helpful strategy. Contacting your alumni career services center (or alumni relations department) may unearth some peers who will tell you their story, and with whom you can test out the rationale for your career transition.

There are resources available for more help with this process. Bob Gardella of HBS Alumni Career Services has created a guide to job transitions entitled, *The Harvard Business School Guide to Finding Your Next Job*. Though not nonprofit-specific, it provides helpful advice about the process, offers tips on selling yourself, and lists various resources available for help at this stage. Several executive-search firms specialize in the nonprofit sector, such as A.T. Kearney's Executive Search Practice, and smaller firms such as E. Caitlen Donneley and Hendrick & Struggles.

A few things to keep in mind if you are considering a "later-life transition":

- It helps significantly to have volunteered and/or served on boards (or to have done pro-bono work) before you attempt to make a transition to nonprofit management. You can't just say "here I am" and slide into a senior management position. James Abruzzo, managing director of A.T. Kearney's Executive Search and Nonprofit practices, looks for executives who have served on nonprofit boards or worked as volunteers and thus "understand the complex culture."

- In making the transition, you need to keep potential cultural differences in mind. Nonprofits are mission-driven, and many of the staff members are program people rather than business people. Furthermore, defining the customer is slightly more difficult, because you have to think about both the funders who make your work possible and the community members for whom you are providing services. The government is also often an involved stakeholder, more so than in the private sector.

- Adjusting to your new role can be difficult. You have to balance your management acumen with your commitment to the cause. Some former for-profit business-people overemphasize the business aspects without sufficient respect for the cause; others come to nonprofits because they believe in the cause but then forget everything they know about management. In addition, Abruzzo notes that the shift from board member to executive director can be especially tricky, because "you go from colleague to employee" in the eyes of the rest of the board, which may be a difficult transition to make.

- "Some for-profit executives have a false impression of nonprofits that underestimates the vision, skills, and challenges of nonprofit leaders and managers. This leads them to believe that they are automatically qualified to go right to the top of the ladder. In reality, this is

not the common path to nonprofit leadership," comments Pat Brandes of the United Way. "Nonprofit executives have a network of very talented nonprofit managers to fill potential senior management positions, so when someone with for-profit senior management experience expects to walk in and be a nonprofit leader, he or she has to do a great job of convincing me that they would offer more."

- One word of caution: do not think that moving to the nonprofit world is a viable "escape strategy" from your current job. If you think about the move this way, you won't be happy with your new position, and most likely you will not be effective either.

KURT KENWORTH

Moving to nonprofit work at age sixty-five

Kurt Kenworth (Harvard Business School, MBA 1958) is a project director at the National Council on the Aging's (NCOA) Los Angeles office. He oversees the implementation in Los Angeles of a national partnership between NCOA and the Department of Labor (DOL). Through this program, DOL provides funds to NCOA and other national contractors, who in turn use the funds to place and pay people fifty-five or older to work in community service agencies for twenty hours a week. According to Kenworth, both parties benefit—the service agency is provided with a free worker, and the senior is provided with valuable skills training and a small salary.

The National Council on the Aging is a center of leadership and nationwide expertise in the issues of aging. As a private, nonprofit association founded in 1950 and headquartered in Washington, D.C., NCOA has a diverse membership of qualified information intermediaries for older adults, including community-based service providers, consumer and labor groups, businesses, government agencies, religious groups, and volunteer organizations. Kenworth's program is one of a number of NCOA initiatives.

Kenworth came to NCOA after a successful career in the manufacturing industry. He left manufacturing at age sixty-five (after forty years in the field) and began networking in the Los Angeles area for a job in a new career field. "When I left business school, I was mostly interested in the marketing and manufacturing of indus-

trial products." He began his career in that field and eventually became CEO of his own manufacturing company. When Kenworth came to NCOA, "I switched from the world of quality control and raw materials into the world of human relations. For years I thought I was a 'thing' person and not a 'people' person. I was wrong."

Kenworth says that his MBA was helpful in a "door-opener" capacity. He notes, "In the interview I floated the idea that hiring me would be an experiment to see if my skills as a manager and leader in the private sector were transferable to the social sector. NCOA took a chance to find out."

"Both the need and the opportunity for MBAs in the social sector are tremendous," says Kenworth. First, MBAs have opportunities to "save the ship" and turn around nonprofits that are in need of professional managers. Second, the opportunity to "fast track" through an organization in the social sector is greater than in the for-profit sector: "The big appeal in the community-service sector is that you have a better chance to rise to the top sooner."

Kenworth faces many day-to-day challenges in the senior citizen employment placement program he runs—including convincing companies to hire elderly workers. "A lot of big companies give lip-service to diversity, but then when the hiring is done down at the local level they don't hire seniors. Instead they hire young people and spend a lot of money training them and then they leave. There was a study done at Harvard that shows that seniors actually learn faster and are more reliable and more dependable as employees. Because of their maturity and experience, older people intuitively understand what facts are important to learn whereas young people try to learn everything. Corporations realize that seniors are a good investment, but more often than not they don't implement the plans to carry out that realization."

When a company does hire an older person, Kenworth feels a strong sense of gratification: "On a personal level, I have found the work at NCOA very satisfying. The reward is immeasurable when you have a participant in a program who gets placed and is really happy and grateful."

Kenworth notes that while he enjoys the day-to-day challenge of serving as a leader in the nonprofit world

and receives great personal satisfaction, a major downside of the nonprofit world is the pay: "Generally speaking, nonprofits can't pay as much because they can't afford it. It's not a criticism of them to say they don't have professional management. They just can't afford it." However, Kenworth adds that he is compensated fairly well and that certain nonprofits are able to offer more competitive pay. Further, Kenworth's six children are grown, which limits his financial obligations.

Kenworth advises students seeking a job in the social sector to find one whose mission fits with their personal desires. Further, he advocates networking: "Tell everyone you can think of and their friends of your availability and interest. I didn't know anything about NCOA when I began searching, and now I feel like it was my lifelong calling."

Starting Your Own Organization

Many of you are entrepreneurs at heart and have serious thoughts about starting your own nonprofit or social enterprise organization. Starting a new social enterprise involves many of the same challenges as start-ups in any field and often more. More and more MBAs (and non-MBAs) have been starting their own social enterprise organizations in recent years, as you will read in the accompanying profiles. John Rice (Harvard Business

School, MBA 1992), founder of Management Leadership for Tomorrow (see profile in chapter 5), comments: "Never underestimate the commitment required to start something from scratch, and be prepared to make sacrifices if that is what you want to do. If you want to develop something new, try to get an equally committed partner to do it with you. And do it sooner rather than later, as it becomes more and more difficult to do the more advanced you get in your career and family life."

ANDREA SILBERT

Helping women become entrepreneurs

Andrea Silbert (Harvard Business School, MBA 1992) is the executive director of the Center for Women & Enterprise (CWE), a nonprofit educational organization whose mission is to empower women to become economically self-sufficient and prosperous through entrepreneurship. The center provides comprehensive business assistance and resources to women who are starting and/or growing their own businesses, including multiweek courses, full-day conferences and other shorter workshops, networking opportunities, and ongoing consulting to clients with whom they develop

deep and lasting relationships. CWE also has two new initiatives, a pilot program that targets women on welfare and the Venture Center, an initiative to help rapidly growing businesses access growth capital.

Silbert herself is an accomplished entrepreneur. She launched CWE in October of 1995, and the organization grew quickly, serving well over 1,000 entrepreneurs by 1998. CWE now serves nearly 600 women per year, many of whom are repeat clients. "My vision is that we will become the most comprehensive and effective business development center in the country—a model for national replication," says Silbert. "But the biggest challenge I face is how to financially support growth. In a for-profit business if you have a good product it pays for itself. In my business, the better your product, the more funding you need. The need for fund-raising never ends."

An entrepreneur at heart, Silbert ran Harvard Student Agencies as an undergraduate and received a deferred acceptance to HBS during her senior year. She spent the next two years in mergers and acquisitions (M&A) at Morgan Stanley (now Morgan Stanley Dean Witter & Company) but found that "investment banking just wasn't connected to my core values." She then spent a year in Costa Rica researching and writing cases about international economic development before starting a joint degree program at HBS and KSG. "I spent my first summer at the World Bank, which also wasn't a good fit." But the next summer, Silbert found Cultural Survival, a nonprofit helping indigenous people harvest Brazil nuts in the Amazon. "I had a wild summer . . . and by the end I knew I would pursue a career directly helping low-income women."

Fresh out of business school, Silbert won an Echoing Green Foundation grant to help Brazilian "street girls" start their own businesses. After a year and a half of

"My job is incredibly challenging and fun— and on top of all that, spiritually rewarding."

difficult work in an economically unstable environment, Silbert's mission had become even more clear: "I was going to start a center for women entrepreneurs." A year later CWE was born.

Though Silbert committed early on to a career in social enterprise, finding other like-minded MBAs to join the center has not been easy. "Hiring is always a challenge. I can't afford to compete with the for-profit companies for talented people, especially high-powered MBAs. But I can offer more than a big paycheck. We attract talented people because we have a powerful and meaningful vision, but the 'call to action' for social enterprise is more than 'doing good work.' My job is incredibly challenging and fun—and on top of all that, spiritually rewarding."

Having been to business school has helped Silbert immensely in her entrepreneurial pursuits. "Though I learned the nuts and bolts of running a business on the job, the MBA program taught me to be systematic and analytical in my thinking, to approach problems with a clear methodology, and to ask the right questions." She also encourages other MBAs to enter the field. "Working as a manager in the sector is an incredibly rich and exciting experience. You will never get the same level of responsibility as quickly in the corporate sector, or the growth opportunities, or the opportunity to be entrepreneurial so early in your career."

STACEY BOYD

Bringing management skills to education

"I have the heart of an educator and the systematic way of looking at things of an MBA," comments Stacey Boyd (Harvard Business School, MBA 1997). As founding director of the Academy of the Pacific Rim, a charter school in Boston, Boyd has found a way to blend her passion and her business skills to create tremendous value in the social sector.

Boyd's career path has been a whirlwind of education and business-related projects. While writing her college thesis on school choice she became convinced that choice between mediocre and poor schools wasn't really choice at all—schools were in serious need of reform. Fascinated by the Japanese educational system, Boyd applied to teach in Japan for a year, and while there, researched elements of education applicable to the U.S. system. At the end of the year, she saw a newspaper article about an innovative new business called the Edison Project in the United States. The project planned to build a private network of schools that educated students at the same or lower cost than the U.S. public schools. Boyd wrote to the founder and was hired as a research associate to build "the New American School."

"Working for the Edison Project was a huge part of my growth, because it enabled me to really figure out what it was about education that I thought needed to be changed. Plus, I worked with a group of very bright people, and I realized that the start-up environment was definitely where I wanted to be."

Two years later, Boyd began a joint degree at HBS and KSG. Midway through the program she worked on a project with Education Partners, a for-profit company in the field of contract management of the public schools. Once again, Boyd put her mind to work on designing a better school, which piqued her interest in the emerging charter school movement. A few weeks before classes began for her final year of school, Boyd came across the charter for the Academy of the Pacific Rim. Rather than take a week or two of vacation, Boyd contacted the chairman of the proposed school, and at the end of her last day at Education Partners, she hopped a red-eye flight back to Boston to work with the board of the academy.

"Originally the academy was going to open that fall. But then a few things went wrong with the building site and the proposed headmaster of the school, and the board realized that we would have to wait a year to open it. I agreed to work with the board on the plan during the year. Then, before I knew it, I was the director of the academy!"

That year of planning was an extremely hectic one for Boyd, as she finished two master's degrees and started a new business—a complex process requiring coordination with a large number of stakeholders in government, education, business, and the general community. "So many things had to happen, from securing a facility, to managing the transportation we would provide, to recruiting staff and students, to developing the curriculum, to dealing with human resources policy and management structure."

As a charter school (an independent public school), the academy is free of traditional public school regulations but is held strictly accountable for results in order to have its five-year charter renewed. "Our goal as a charter school is to show what you can do with the same resources as public schools, and the same set of kids, but free from bureaucracy."

The idea of the academy is to "combine the respect for education and discipline found in the East with the emphasis on individuality and diversity found in the West." The school has several unique elements, including extensive parent involvement (parents or sponsors and children have to sign a contract before beginning school); a program that combines practical and work skills, health and fitness, culture and the arts, and character education; extended school hours and a longer school year than the typical public school; and detailed performance objectives for students and teachers alike. Teachers are given significant preparation time and technology to support their work, and professional development opportunities throughout the year, but are also held strictly accountable to performance goals and paid and promoted accordingly. The most talked-about innovation may be the academy's money-back guarantee: the school will turn over the equivalent of the funds it receives from the state for each child who fails the Massachusetts Comprehensive Assessment System test in the tenth and eleventh grades.

Boyd shares several reflections on the process of building a school. "First of all, it's important to remember that this is a marathon. You have to pace yourself and do everything you can not to hit the wall. Champions are born in the middle of the race." Second, though the classroom is about education, business thinking has to influence all the systems that surround the classroom. "All of the HBS cases—even the awful ones about meat slaughtering and packaging—really do apply. They teach you the underlying principles about running an or-

> *"First of all, it's important to remember that this is a marathon. You have to pace yourself and do everything you can not to hit the wall. Champions are born in the middle of the race."*

ganization." The application of business principles to the academy is clear through the concept of performance measurement, the use of information management software, and the design of incentives for parents and teachers alike, among many other aspects of the management process.

Creating change in an entrenched system of education has not been easy, but Boyd has lived by the educational philosophy of her school, which challenges students with *gambatte*—a Japanese word meaning "persist, or fight to the end." She comments: "The nonprofit world can be frustrating if you don't know why you're doing what you're doing. Education in particular is a huge 'industry.' If you want to create change in education, you have to define what it is about education that you believe needs to be changed and why, and then bring about that change wholeheartedly." In Boyd's mind, the biggest problem in education was poor management, so she focused on improving the management of schools.

Boyd's entrepreneurial instincts have led her to pursue additional education-focused innovation as well. In 1998 she began the national rollout of an information management system designed for primary and secondary schools. The system—Achieve (developed and distributed through Boyd's company, the Learning Contract)—helps schools track what has been taught and what has been learned. "It's so simple," says Boyd, "yet until now there was no tool to help teachers do this."

According to Boyd, the hardest part about nonprofit management is "changing the perceptions of those that work in schools and nonprofits to convince them that doing good is not incompatible with running an efficient and professional organization." The Academy of the Pacific Rim and the Achieve Software seem to be two steps in the right direction.

Steps Along the Way

If you know that you want to be involved in the nonprofit sector—whether right away or much later in life—two major steps along the way will help smooth the transition when you are ready: volunteering for a nonprofit and serving on a nonprofit board of directors. Each of these activities deepens your understanding of the critical issues such organizations face, helps you develop contacts in the nonprofit community, and increases your overall credibility as a potential nonprofit leader. And it's never too early to get started.

Volunteering

Community service is valuable in its own right, whether or not you have any interest in a social enterprise career. However, if you want to work in a nonprofit organization now or in the future, or plan to be involved as a board member without making a career of nonprofit work, volunteer experiences are extremely valuable stepping stones. Volunteering lets you learn more about how nonprofits work and stimulates your thoughts about contributions you can make as a nonprofit manager. Equally important (especially for MBAs), consistent volunteer involvement sends a strong signal to nonprofit organizations of your commitment to and understanding of the field. Without this background, you will be a less attractive candidate for nonprofit management positions at any stage in life.

You might also think about the volunteer experience as a personal development opportunity. Try to find an opportunity that offers you the chance to use and explore skills that you may not develop in your full-time position, as well as to learn more about the culture of a nonprofit organization and to interact with both staff and management team members.

So, how do you get involved? The easiest way is to work with an existing volunteer organization—such as your alumni club's volunteer group (graduate and/or undergraduate). Many corporations have volunteer programs or relationships with nonprofit organizations, and you can contact the human resources department or the director of community relations to learn about them. Professional service firms (for example, consulting or law firms) often do pro-bono work in their communities. You can go through community organizations such as the United Way's Voluntary Action Centers (located around the nation), or just talk to a friend involved in community service.

A few questions to ask yourself before committing to a volunteer activity:

- How much time do you want to commit (and how much *can* you commit)? How regularly can you commit (once a week, once a month, sporadically)?

- How do you want to help? By applying business skills (consulting, financial management help)? Through more direct service (tutoring, mentoring)?

- Do you want to work for an organization that focuses on any specific community issues, such as children or education?

- Do you want to volunteer with a group or on your own?

For more information on volunteering, see chapter 6, the Resource Road Map.

CARTER ROBERTS

From volunteer to nonprofit manager

Carter Roberts (Harvard Business School, MBA 1988) spent several years after business school in the corporate sector. He worked for several companies, including Procter & Gamble, Dun and Bradstreet, and the Gillette Company, but found himself spending all of his free time climbing mountains. After a point he realized that he also wanted to spend more of his workday "on issues I cared about." So he began to volunteer at The Nature Conservancy (TNC), a nonprofit environmental organization, and then progressed from volunteer, to manager of the Boston office, to his current position as TNC's vice president and Central America regional director. Roberts now manages seven TNC offices in the United States and Central America to advance the organization's work with partners in Panama, Costa Rica, Nicaragua, Honduras, and Guatemala.

This path from volunteer to nonprofit executive is not an uncommon one. As Roberts advises, "It is hard to make the jump from the for-profit world to the nonprofit world unless someone knows you well. Volunteering is a great way to make that happen."

The Nature Conservancy's mission is to preserve plants, animals, and natural communities that represent the diversity of life on Earth by protecting the lands and waters they need to survive. Among environmental organizations TNC fills a unique niche: preserving habitats and species by buying the lands and waters they need to survive. The Nature Conservancy operates the largest private system of nature sanctuaries in the world—more than 1,500 preserves in the United States alone. Some are "postage-stamp size," others cover thousands of acres. All of them safeguard imperiled species of plants and animals.

TNC is truly an international organization with interests in North and South America and the Pacific. The largest conservation nonprofit in the world, TNC's annual budget of $500 million covers over 250 offices and approximately 2,300 employees. Results to date include the protection of over ten million acres in the United States and 25 million acres in Latin America.

Roberts notes, "I am working with people to literally save the world—or at least a little bit of it. I get to spend time in amazing rain forests and coral reefs with an amazing range of people. Today I am meeting with the president of Costa Rica, and next week I will be working with Mayan people in Guatemala." Furthermore, "The quality of personnel here is very, very high. We have several Ph.D.s, MBAs, and J.D.s who work very long hours and have a great time together." He adds that he has "tons of independence and responsibility" and is only limited by "how much money I can raise" to support his activities. There are some frustrations, although Roberts characterizes them as minimal. "The lengthy decision-making process that sometimes occurs" is perhaps the most frustrating aspect of his work.

The premier challenge facing TNC is how to discover and implement creative ways to resolve economic and environmental conflict. However, the MBA experience prepared Roberts by helping him develop a facility with numbers, budgets, organizations, and strategic planning.

When asked for advice for MBAs, Roberts echoes the sentiments of his peers: "Life is too short. Before you get old and gray, do something you love."

Board Membership

Board membership is another powerful way to have impact on the community, to leverage your business skills, and to meet other business and community leaders who share some of your community interests. Serving on a board is both an honor and a serious responsibility—you will have legal and fiduciary responsibilities for the organization just as board members of for-profit organizations do. Nonprofit management and staff look to board members for strategic and operational guidance, fund-raising assistance, and general and legal oversight.

Becoming a board member is often a function of connections. When an organization decides that it needs to form or expand its board (or fill a vacated seat), the current board and senior management rely heavily on word of mouth and relationships to find new members. Often, nonprofit executives select board members who will together meet three critical needs: (1) a specific skill set or range of expertise including financial management, legal knowledge, and/or programmatic vision; (2) an ability to enhance the organization's fund-raising capacity through their own donations, connections to larger circles, and creative fund-raising ability; and (3) a diverse overall board membership, including geographic, racial, gender, and socioeconomic diversity. To keep the organization in touch with its mission, a constituent voice may also be included on the board.

Some "broker" organizations exist to help match potential board members with organizations in need of them. The United Way BoardBank is one of these. Your graduate and undergraduate alumni clubs may also be able to help. And you can talk with current board members to let them know of your interest; they will probably be asked to make recommendations at some point.

Before accepting a seat on a board, you should do some due diligence and make sure that you are serious about the commitment you are about to make. Talk with current board members and the senior management team to learn about the organization's mission, key challenges, financial status, and expectations of the board. Some boards are extremely active, others are much less so.

For more information on board membership, see chapter 6, Resource Road Map.

PROFESSOR WARREN McFARLAN

Active board membership

Professor F. Warren McFarlan (Harvard Business School, MBA 1961, DBA 1965), senior associate dean and director of external relations for Harvard Business School, has been an active board member of several nonprofit organizations in two areas: independent schooling and health care. Professor McFarlan's nonprofit board experience began when he became a member of the board of trustees of Belmont Day School, an independent school in Massachusetts for prekindergartners to sixth-graders. He later served as chairman of the board at Belmont Day for four years. Professor McFarlan was also on the board of the Dana Hall School (an independent school for girls in grades six to twelve) for eleven years, including four years as chairman of the board. He recently became a member of the board of Winsor School, an independent school for fifth- to twelfth-graders. In addition, he was a trustee of Mount Auburn Hospital and served as chairman of the board for three and a half years. During his tenure as chairman, Mount Auburn merged into Care-Group, a health-care organization that now includes Mount Auburn Hospital, Beth Israel Deaconess Medical Center, New England Baptist Hospital, Deaconess-Glover Hospital, Deaconess-Waltham Hospital, and Deaconess-Nashoba Hospital. Professor McFarlan has been on CareGroup's board since its founding and currently serves as board treasurer and on the executive committee.

Because each of these organizations faced unique challenges, Professor McFarlan's board experiences have been quite diverse. At Belmont Day School, the task facing the board was to "manage prosperity." Independent schools were growing in Massachusetts in response to the passage of Proposition 2-½, which capped property taxes, thereby limiting funds available for public schools. Professor McFarlan notes, "Lots of cash was flowing in and we needed to make the right investments." In contrast, during his time as chairman at Dana Hall School there was a need to "manage through adversity, since independent girls' education was not in favor." Finally, the board at Mount Auburn Hospital needed to plan and look ahead in response to a rapidly changing health-care environment. "Mount Auburn had experienced 125 years of independent existence and had run surpluses for the past decade. However, the changing medical, legal, and political context meant that there would not be another 125 years of independence. The challenge was to mobilize the board, the administration, and the physicians to confront the issues while we were still strong" (see Harvard Business School Case 9-397-083, "Mt. Auburn Hospital").

In addition to his nonprofit board memberships, Professor McFarlan is a member of several corporate boards (Computer Science Corporation, Pioneer Hi-Bred International Inc., and Providian Financial Corporation). He notes many similarities between corporate and nonprofit boards—and some deep and fundamental differences. First, "mission is dominant in the social sector. This makes financial management much more complicated because of the potential for conflict between mission and finances. Core activities can be 'loss leaders.' A corporate board might recommend 'cleaning up' these activities, but cleaning them up in a social sector organization could destroy the organization's essence." A second key difference is the relationship between the nonexecutive chairman of the board and the full-time executive officer (in corporations, one individual often wears the hats of chairman and CEO). Third, the role of a nonprofit board member changes more over time. Typically, time commitment and involvement for a nonprofit board member grow over time with some risk of burnout. Furthermore, while corporate board members are often compensated with cash and stock options, nonprofit board members may be expected to make large contributions. A fourth difference between corporate and nonprofit boards is that nonprofit boards are often larger. This structural feature makes the executive committee very important, but organizations need to be wary of an "upstairs/downstairs" board forming as a result. A final difference Professor McFarlan highlights is that nonprofit boards typically have more turnover than corporate boards. As a result, nonprofit boards need to groom future leaders and be careful of becoming overly dependent on a few individuals.

Professor McFarlan offers several pieces of advice for MBAs interested in becoming effective nonprofit board members. Start by serving on "starter boards"—boards of smaller organizations with small budgets—and then move on to larger, more complex, more sophisticated organizations (alternatively, MBAs might initially get involved by volunteering for larger organizations), he suggests. In terms of effectiveness, Professor McFarlan refers back to the importance of mission. His advice to MBAs: "Listen well. Unless you understand the organization's core values, you risk starting off with your model of the corporate world and being head-over-heels before you know it." Additionally, "nonprofits need a variety of skills—community relations skills, financial skills, and development and philanthropy skills." Professor McFarlan recommends taking the time to understand why each of the different board members are there and how they contribute.

"Listen well. Unless you understand the organization's core values, you risk starting off with your model of the corporate world and being head-over-heels before you know it."

Professor McFarlan has found his nonprofit board memberships very rewarding. "I get a lot of enjoyment helping these enterprises turn around and meet the challenges that face them. I see board membership as an opportunity to make an impact on things you think are important."

CHAPTER THREE

The Job-Search Process

Overview

As you are aware, the job-search process for graduating MBAs seeking nonprofit/social enterprise jobs is much less clear-cut than traditional "corporate" jobs. Why? Many things distinguish the nonprofit job search:

- Nonprofits are not traditional MBA recruiters. They get their people more through word of mouth and networking than through recruiting channels such as on-campus visits.

- Even if they do work with schools to recruit employee talent, nonprofits have a harder time predicting open positions and have fewer positions open than do consulting firms or large corporations. In addition, nonprofits do not have "recruiting calendars" that fit neatly with an academic calendar.

- Nonprofits have less experience working with MBAs and less money to offer, so they rarely actively seek MBAs and often shy away from them. You will have to be much more proactive in your pursuit of social enterprise jobs than will your classmates looking at consulting, banking, brand management, and other more common fields of interest.

- Job descriptions may be less clearly defined, and the recruiting and interviewing processes may be much less structured with nonprofit organizations than with corporate recruiters.

- The nonprofit search will more often than not be a networked job search. You will be more likely to find your job by talking with friends, peers, and those in the field than by looking for a formal job posting.

Getting Started

Background Research

Do a Little Soul-Searching
Take some time to think about what you really enjoy and why you want to work in social enterprise. You probably already did a lot of this when writing out your career aspirations. Here are a few things to think about:

- What subject(s) do you really care about? Is it child care, environmental concerns, homelessness, education, the arts? (See the subsector sections in chapter 5 for more detail on several potential areas of interest.)

- What functions do you enjoy? Marketing, finance, general management, fund-raising, human resources, communications?

- What organizational characteristics appeal to you? Small? Large? Specific geography? Age of peers? Entrepreneurial? Established?

Get a Sense of Potential Job Opportunities at On-Campus Events
- Pay attention when social sector leaders visit your classes; guests can be great sources of information or great contacts for jobs.

- Think about doing course projects focused on nonprofits, or do a volunteer consulting project to learn more about organizations of interest and to develop a network in the field. Many business schools have clubs that organize volunteer consulting projects with local nonprofits.

- Talk to people: The best way to gather information is to talk to others already in the field, those considering it, or board members. Talk to professors, classmates, guest speakers, friends in the field, etc.

Find a Job-Search Buddy
Pool resources by getting together with a group of other nonprofit job seekers. Your school's nonprofit club or membership in Students for Responsible Business (now, NetImpact) may help with this.

Creating a Hit List
Now that you have a sense of your interests and the world of opportunities, *create a hit list* of organizations you might like to pursue (or at least learn more about). Use the subsector sections in chapter 5, your business school

cases, the Web, and your friends and social enterprise contacts to help develop this list. The hit list and information search process will be an iterative one—the first list is just a starting point.

Once you have your hit list, go to the Web or print resources for more detailed information. The *Nonprofit Times* <www.nptimes.com>, *GuideStar* <www.guide star.org>, and the *Chronicle of Philanthropy* <www. philanthropy.com> are all useful resources that include links to other nonprofit sites. Also see the Resource Road Map in chapter 6.

See the Students for Responsible Business (NetImpact) Web site. SRB organizes and publicizes summer and postMBA social enterprise positions (for members only). For information and listings, see the SRB Web site at <www.srb.org>.

Informational Interviews

Informational interviews provide an honest, first-person perspective on the type of organization you're interested in without the pressure of an actual "hire me" interview. Alumni are usually willing to spend a bit of time with you for this purpose. The clearer you are on your objectives and "target market" before approaching contacts, the more you will get out of these conversations. In addition to helping you learn more about an organization, informational interviews will help broaden your network of social enterprise contacts.

Contacting Organizations

Cover Letters and Resumes

Many publications provide guidance on cover letters and resumes, which will be helpful for the nonprofit as well as the for-profit job search. A few key points follow:

- If possible, your cover letter should make reference to how you found out about the organization, noting a personal reference if at all possible (for example, "Professor Nonprofit who is on the board suggested I write to you . . .").

- Getting a personal introduction, or even having someone mention to the executive director that you may call, will be very helpful.

- In your cover letter, emphasize why you are interested and any relevant experience, since organizations may not have experience working with MBAs.

- Just as you would tailor your resume for high-tech or consulting positions, you will have to tailor your resume for social enterprise. Reemphasize volunteer ex-

periences that you may have taken off your resume when you came to business school. Your resume should mention your involvement in social enterprise endeavors, including business school (and undergraduate) experiences such as tutoring, volunteer consulting, organizing community-service events, coursework, etc. You may also want to reword your corporate experience in plain English for non-Wall Street audiences.

Interviews

Before the Interview

- Make sure you've read the organization's annual report and visited its Web site (if it has one), and familiarize yourself with its mission and the challenges it faces. If possible, talk with some people who know the organization to get a better perspective before the interview. Also make sure you've done your homework and have opinions about the overall field in which it works.

- You also want to go into the interview knowing how to articulate your interests and the strengths and unique capabilities you will bring to the organization (including how your MBA will help). Make sure to bring up your relevant volunteer and other experience, as well as your passion for the issues.

On the Day

- What should you wear? Nonprofit dress codes vary widely—some are corporate business attire, some are very casual, most are in between. Try to get a sense of the organization before you go (you can call the secretary of the person who is going to interview you), and err on the slightly conservative side by dressing up a level. Even when you dress "corporate," avoid the Wall Street power suits.

- What will they ask? It won't be a case interview, but interviewers will still be looking for you to demonstrate your knowledge and capabilities. They may probe your knowledge about the field in addition to asking about your skill set, especially if your prior experience in the field appears limited.

- They may also question you about why you went to business school and, if you do not have prior nonprofit experience, why you want to work in a nonprofit organization.

- Be prepared to discuss strategic issues they are facing and to have a point of view.

- Take advantage of the interview day to learn more about the culture of the organization while you're there. You need to learn about the organization and the other employees as much as they need to learn about you to determine if there will be a good fit.

Follow-up
- Send a thank-you note. For nonprofits, this can be a meatier letter than what you might send to a consulting firm. You may want to reflect on the conversation and describe the role you think you could play in the organization, or give your point of view on a strategic issue it is facing.

Evaluating Opportunities

Especially with a summer internship, having a clearly defined project and role is critical to a successful experience. The summer is too short to spend the first few weeks scoping out how you might help. Plus, having a tangible end-product or contribution to the organization at the end of the summer adds to your own feeling of accomplishment. For these reasons, established programs such as SRB internships provide potentially better learning experiences.

The opportunity should use your current set of skills, but should also be a venue to grow and gain new skills. Good career opportunities provide room for development and advance you down the path you want to pursue.

As with any job—for-profit or nonprofit—having a mentor in the organization adds tremendous value. Make sure there is someone who will be committed to setting aside time to dedicate to your development. Without a mentor (who could be a board member, if you are taking a senior position at a nonprofit later in your career) you may be setting yourself up for disappointment.

You should also make sure that you fit with the culture, and that you will feel comfortable working there. In nonprofit work, many MBAs have found that one indication of potential culture fit is whether or not there are other MBAs in the organization. For example, Ted Preston (profiled in chapter 2) found The Community Builders to be a "very market-driven" organization. "I feel extremely comfortable in this culture. There are several other MBAs at TCB . . . and we work well together."

Beyond fit, you should make sure that the organization understands the value of having an MBA. Some value MBAs but might try to pigeonhole you in finance. If the organization doesn't see an MBA as a valuable contributor to strategic issues beyond finance, the job most likely will not be a great experience.

Salary/Funding Considerations

Financial considerations play a significant role in many job decisions, especially when you are the "proud owner" of business school loans. In general, social enterprise jobs will not pay as well as corporate jobs, although salaries have become much more reasonable in recent years (see chapter 2 for more details). However, don't fool yourself—you will never make a salary comparable to your consulting or investment banking friends, no matter how senior you become in the organization. While the financial aspect of the job decision ultimately depends on your personal situation, you can tap into several sources of financial support.

A word of advice from the COO of the United Way of Massachusetts Bay: "You need to separate your sense of personal worth from your actual salary. While you should think about how much you need, and about what is fair within the nonprofit sector, you have to realize that your salary will not be indicative of your personal value and contribution to the organization. It is simply an indication of how much the organization can afford to pay for the skills you bring to them."

Sources of Financial Support

The following list describes some of the fellowship/funding opportunities most relevant for MBAs. For a more comprehensive list of fellowships (including those for college students and current nonprofit staff and executives) see <www.idealist.org/career/fellowship.htm>.

- Echoing Green Foundation Fellowships support social entrepreneurs—at both the undergraduate and graduate levels—as they launch innovative social programs and focus on raising additional funds to support their new organizations. Participants receive $20,000 to $30,000 annually along with technical assistance for a start-up project anywhere in the world. For more information on Echoing Green, see its Web site at <www.echoing green.org>.

- The Fund for Social Entrepreneurs, sponsored by Youth Service America, provides seed capital, stipends, and professional development to entrepreneurs age twenty-one to thirty-five who are starting an innovative, youth-service, nonprofit organization. For more information, see its Web site at <www.servenet.org>.

- Kauffman Social Entrepreneur Internship Program Fellowships subsidize MBA students during the summer work experience to allow students with an interest in social entrepreneurial ventures to take jobs at such organizations without the usual financial sacrifice this would impose. Kauffman works with several business schools, so check with your career services office for more information, or see the foundation's Web site at <www.emkf.org>.

- Ashoka Fellows is an international nonprofit fellowship program that supports social entrepreneurs in Asia, Latin America, Africa, and East Central Europe. Ashoka Fellowships fund projects with a broad social impact on issues such as health, environment, education, legal rights, women, children, and development. For more information, see the Web site at <www.ashoka.org>.

- The Warren Weavers Fellows Program, a year-long program sponsored by the Rockefeller Foundation, of-fers $45,000 to $60,000 in stipends to participants, who spend a year working on projects of interest relevant to the foundation's funding areas. For more information, call (212) 852-8407.

- The Public Interest Pioneers Program, a program of the Stern Family Fund, provides seed grants of $50,000 to $100,000 to spark the creation of new organizations. The fund searches for individuals with meaningful experiences who are prepared to launch innovative government and corporate accountability projects. For more information, see <www.essential.org/stern/#pioneer> or call (703) 527-6692.

JENNIFER MIN

Making a connection through the Society and Enterprise course

Jennifer Min (Harvard Business School, MBA 1999) was so intrigued by the Timberland/City Year case discussed during a required first-year Society and Enterprise course at HBS that she introduced herself to Priscilla Twan, deputy director of national affairs of City Year. "I knew of City Year before the class, and when we read the case I got much more interested. I was particularly curious about how they measured or defined success for their service projects for both corps members and service partners. After I asked Priscilla a few questions about City Year, she asked me about my background, and I left with her name and number in case I wanted to pursue an opportunity to work there."

Min had planned to work in either consulting or high tech for the summer, but also felt that after many years of volunteering at schools and after-school programs, she wanted some "real" work experience in a nonprofit organization to be at least part of her summer internship. "I knew that my summer associate position (at Bain & Company Inc., a management consulting firm) wouldn't start until mid-June. So I called Priscilla to see if there were any opportunities for me to help out at City Year. Our initial conversation over coffee turned into a five-week paid ($100 per week) internship, during which I worked on City Year's New Site Development Strategy."

"I, Jennifer Min, with all of three weeks of City Year under my belt, was in charge of new site development."

At City Year, Min designed and created a "Toolkit for Bringing City Year to Your Community." Historically, City Year had not had a formal process for identifying or evaluating prospective cities to start new City Year programs. The organization had expanded successfully to ten cities since its original founding in Boston ten years ago. Each expansion city had been identified and supported mainly through one or two "champions" either internal or external to City Year. Over the years, however, these individuals had become a diminishing resource and City Year had difficulty providing appropriate resources to support and sustain the new programs. Thus City Year was in search of a more systematic approach to "prospecting" new cities.

"I spent my first two weeks interviewing former City Year champions and trying to determine what worked and what did not in terms of new site development. I also spoke with start-up team members to try and ascertain what City Year as an organization could improve to execute and support the new programs. My third week consisted of working with City Year leaders to discuss my findings and develop a how-to tool kit for new sites."

Throughout the first three weeks Min also contacted a number of representatives from different cities who had previously contacted City Year about new site development. She answered their questions and provided them with information, and then invited them to City Year's annual national conference (CYZYGY).

"The conference became another whole project in itself and the most challenging aspect of my internship. I was designated new site development coordinator and was responsible for all new site delegates. I was asked to essentially 'sell' City Year and serve as the main point of contact and City Year 'expert' for the new site delegates. I, Jennifer Min, with all of three weeks of City Year under my belt, was in charge of new site development. Learning as I executed, I developed a three-day program for the delegates to expose them to City Year and offer them ample opportunity to meet and speak with any City Year leader, corps member, or staff person." The fourth week of Min's internship was the actual conference at John Carroll University in Cleveland, Ohio, "which was an amazing and amazingly hectic week!" And in her final week, Min followed up with the new

site delegates who had attended CYZYGY and organized her work so that the next new site development coordinator could pick up where she left off.

"My summer experience at City Year exceeded my goals and expectations. It was an exciting, challenging, and fun five weeks. The learning and exposure that I gained in that short period of time was more than I have learned in one or two years with other organizations." That said, Min was struck by the resource struggle facing nonprofits like City Year. The flip side of the great amount of responsibility she was given: "there was no one else there with the time to work on new site development, and yet site development is a fairly high priority for the organization. I was a little worried about what would happen when I left, because no one had been given specific responsibility to take over my work. And yet they have gotten this far, always with the same struggle—which is a testament to the City Year staff's dedication and commitment."

What Nonprofit Employers Look For

"Think about what skills you bring to the sector that we don't have. Often that means marketing or finance, or broader strategic capabilities. These are the best entry points, and then once you're a known quantity in the organization you can branch out to more program-related work."

—PAT BRANDES
Chief Operating Officer, United Way of Massachusetts Bay

"I look for sincere passion, since that translates into commitment. I want someone with the ability to think big about an initiative and its potential but execute effectively in small steps."

—JOHN RICE
(Harvard Business School, MBA 1992)
Founder, Management Leadership for Tomorrow

"When I see an MBA, I know that they have the skills to work here. What I care more about is their attitude. I look for someone who is open-minded, who can get along with my staff and the kids in my program, who is committed to helping people. That type of person will fit into the culture and will do well here."

—JENNIFER BROWN SIMON
(Harvard Business School, MBA 1994)
Executive Director, Washington Tennis and
Education Foundation

"I look for two things. First, an appropriate skill set, including marketing, people management, project management, analytic capabilities, etc. Second, a commitment to the cause, beyond the business issues at hand—I want the executive who has volunteered in the past, not someone sick of the corporate rat race and trying to find a way out.

—JAMES ABRUZZO
Managing Director, A.T. Kearney's Executive Search
and Nonprofit practices

"I look for someone who both has the business skills and is driven by the social purpose. The business skills are key because we need someone who can help us build the company, market the organization, and really help take us to the next level. However, it's equally important that the person is mission-driven. He or she should be able to recognize that our mission of tapping into community potential is the business opportunity."

—NEIL SILVERSTON
(Harvard Business School, MBA 1987)
President, WorkSource Staffing Partnership Inc.

"You have to be a lot more proactive with nonprofit organizations than with the for-profit firms. The nonprofits won't be knocking on your door like the consulting firms."

—KIM LEW
(Harvard Business School, MBA 1992)
Portfolio Strategist, Ford Foundation

"Most organizations want to know that you have some content expertise in addition to your business skills. Just having an MBA is not enough to be effective in the nonprofit sector."

—TED PRESTON
(Harvard Business School, MBA 1998)
Director of Educational Programming, The Community Builders Inc.

"I look for people who have diversity of experience, who have a game plan, and who are deliberately going after something. I'm interested in people who have spent time in difficult situations, where they have had to draw on all their talents."

—ANDREW KENDALL
(Harvard Business School, MBA 1988)
Director of Boston Programs, Massachusetts Audubon Society

CHAPTER FOUR

Managing Expectations

If you've never worked in a nonprofit before, a word of warning is warranted: it may be a very different world than the one you're used to. We spent some time talking with alumni in the field to get their sense of the positives and the negatives of working in the sector, as well as advice for how to make the most of your experience.

Key Roles and Positions

Before diving into the positive and negative aspects (see Table 4-1: Pros and Cons of Working in the Social Sector), it may be helpful to see the types of positions that MBAs might hold in social enterprise organizations. Though typical roles in nonprofits are fairly similar to those in a corporation, there are some important distinctions. First, many small organizations take the "chief cook and bottle-washer" approach to responsibilities—meaning everyone does everything possible. Positions also differ depending on the "subsector" in which you are working (for example, foundations have program officers and portfolio managers; community development financial institutions have loan and venture officers, etc.). However, in many organizations you will find the following typical management positions:

- *Executive director (ED):* The ED is another term for CEO or president. EDs generally report directly to the board of directors. If the organization is large enough, there is also a *chief operating officer (COO)* or director of operations. Sometimes the COO role is split into director of operations (covering finance, human resources, and infrastructure) and director of programs (covering management of service programs).

- *Director of development:* Responsible for fund-raising—and often the second most important person in the organization after the ED.

- *Director of marketing/communications:* Similar role to for-profit businesses, with a bit more public relations and communications than the typical marketing manager.

- *Chief financial officer (CFO):* Manages all accounting and grant disbursement, but often has a broader range of responsibilities.

- *Director of MIS:* Manages the information systems, which in many nonprofits may be a little less than leading edge.

- *Program director:* Manages specific programs—probably most comparable to a product manager in a consumer products company.

- *Human resources (HR) director:* In smaller nonprofits, the HR role may fall to the executive director, but many larger organizations have a full-time position.

- *Manager of special projects:* Just what it sounds like—parallel in some ways to strategic planning staff or internal consultants.

MBAs tend to gravitate toward the roles of CEO/COO, CFO, marketing, or special projects. It is harder to make the case for development (fund-raising) or program director unless you have prior experience in the area, but many MBAs have been successful in these areas as well.

Cultural Differences in Nonprofit Organizations

The nonprofit culture is very different from that of the for-profit, and it is that way purposely. Nonprofit organizations tend to fulfill four main functions:

- The production of a product or service in the community

- An outlet for self-expression, where individuals can act on their altruistic ambitions

- A social capital purpose—providing a place for people with common interests to simply come together

- A vehicle for advocacy; not lobbying per se, but a call to society about an important issue

When you enter a nonprofit organization, it is critical to figure out how to accommodate the inherent cultural differences. You have to recognize that the same characteristics that make the nonprofit environment frustrating are also the characteristics that enable it to play a special role in society. You also have to be honest with yourself about the reason you want to work in the field. If you're not mission-driven at all, you will have a very hard time fitting in.

Lisa Schorr (profiled in chapter 2) notes some other cultural differences for MBAs entering the social sector. First, you have to prove yourself in different ways in nonprofit organizations. Your MBA gives you credibility in terms of business skills, but the flip side is that staff in social enterprises may see you differently when you're the only MBA around. "You have to break down their stereotyped expectations by easing into the culture. Staff may hold you at arm's length until they realize that the MBA is only a degree, not a personality type."

Table 4-1

Pros and Cons of Working in the Social Sector

The Pros	The Cons
• Most of the time, people are passionate about what they do. The energy of many vision-driven organizations is compelling.	• The pay is usually less—often much less—than that of many of your classmates. But sometimes the hours are just as long, depending on the situation.
• Potentially, a more diverse group of colleagues, with experiences that will fascinate you.	• There can be more bureaucracy and many fewer resources, making it more difficult to get things done. One MBA alumnus notes, "Sometimes you have to make 'bad' decisions because of resource constraints. The dilemma can be painful."
• The financial bottom line is not the only line that matters; managing the bottom line is simply a requirement to better achieve the mission.	
• The culture is often very sensitive to personal support and positive interactions; mission-driven people have high levels of enthusiasm and energy for what they do.	• There is a continual need for fund-raising. "In a for-profit business, if you have a good product, it pays for itself. In my business, the better your product, the more funding you need," says one MBA in the field.
• You get a tremendous level of responsibility early in your career, and you interact with leaders from all sectors—corporate, government, and community.	

However, it is also important to note that significant differences among various social enterprise organizations can be larger than the differences between community and corporate organizations. A United Way or Boys and Girls Club (large and established) will have a very different culture than a grass-roots organization, and an organization with a staff trained primarily in social services will differ greatly from one with a staff of people with more business training (or an advocacy organization, with significant legal training).

In addition, even if you choose to work in a nonprofit organization, you will often interact with leaders in government, business, and the community. Partnerships are critical to nonprofits' success. Jennifer Min (profiled in chapter 3) notes, "City Year would not be successful if it were not for its corporate sponsors providing credibility and financial support, public sector support in each of its cities, and community support for recruiting and service projects. . . . If any one of those partnerships is weak, there is a big threat of failure." In this area, your strength as an MBA will be your relationships with and ability to talk to partners "on both sides"—the nonprofit staff and service constituents, and potential funders and corporate partners.

Myths and Misconceptions

Nonprofit employees don't work hard. While this may be true in some nonprofit organizations (and some for-profit organizations as well!), the majority of successful nonprofit managers work just as hard or harder than their peers in the corporate world. Jennifer Min (Harvard Business School, MBA 1999) comments: "When I worked at City Year I realized that you can work just as hard and just as long in nonprofit as in for-profit. The difference is—I knew *why* I was doing it *and* I enjoyed it." That said, it is important to note that nonprofit organizations tend to emphasize work-life balance slightly more than their corporate counterparts, and working late is seen more as a means to achieve the mission than a "rite of passage" or "way of life" as it often is on Wall Street. As Desiree Caldwell (Harvard Business School, MBA 1987), executive director of the Concord Museum, comments, "The time demands of a nonprofit job are just as great as in for-profit. I have tons of night events and the board members all have day jobs. I have more flexibility, but nonprofit jobs do eat into your leisure time."

You will only earn about $30,000 per year if you go into nonprofit work. True, there are nonprofit organizations that pay their managers fairly low salaries. However, there are a wide range of opportunities to earn significantly more in nonprofit work (see earlier discussion of salaries in chapter 3). Executive directors recognize that they need MBA skills and must be willing to pay for them, up to a point. But the salary ceilings are significantly lower in nonprofit organizations than in the corporate sector, and there are no big profit-sharing bonuses. Most successful nonprofit leaders are willing to give up some financial remuneration because they truly believe in the mission of the organization.

There are no business skills in nonprofit organizations, and mine won't be valued. While many nonprofits do struggle with lack of management capacity, the sector as a whole has recognized the value of business skills and the need to develop such capacity. More and more MBAs are entering the sector, and initiatives have emerged to strengthen the management capacity of nonMBAs as well. For example, Eureka Communities' Fellowship Program brings together community-based, nonprofit leaders seeking to achieve new standards of excellence. In addition, the distrust of MBAs that once existed in nonprofit organizations has dissolved over the years as more MBAs enter the sector and more nonprofits recognize the need for MBA skills.

I'll work with a limited group of people. Actually, the nonprofit sector provides opportunities to work with a very wide group of people, from the staff, to the board of directors and other stakeholders, to major corporate and government leaders. Because nonprofits often rely on partnerships across the three sectors, you will develop many types of relationships in the natural course of your work.

There's no innovation in the social sector. Actually, innovation is rampant in the social sector. In fact, the many constraints that nonprofits and social purpose organizations face almost force them to be innovative in order to survive, and creativity is definitely valued.

All nonprofits have enthusiastic, passionate employees. While we would like to believe that this is true, the social sector—like the corporate sector—has both "stars" and "duds." The best advice holds true to a job search in any field—look for the best fit by doing appropriate due diligence with people inside and outside the organization.

ANDREW FALENDER

MBA skills make a difference

Andrew Falender (Harvard Business School, MBA 1971), executive director of the Appalachian Mountain Club (AMC), admits "When I entered HBS in 1967, right after I graduated from college, I didn't have the slightest idea about what career I would pursue. What I did know was that I was intrigued by management and leadership issues." Yes, Falender did graduate four years after entering business school: "After my first few months at business school I became frustrated, because while I enjoyed studying management, I lacked a clear sense of how I wanted to use the MBA skills." Falender left business school after his first year to enter the Peace Corps. "While in the Peace Corps I spent a lot of time with a city mayor in the Philippines, who listened to every word I uttered, but did nothing." After two years Falender returned to business school, and since graduation has put his management skills to good use in both the public and

"Finding this opportunity was a matter of timing and luck."

nonprofit sectors. Falender was frustrated by his sense that too many "government and nonprofit resources were being wasted due to the lack of leadership or management capacity." He has tried to change that throughout his career.

During his second year at HBS, Falender took a recruiting trip to Washington, D.C., to interview with the U.S. Department of Health, Education and Welfare, now the separate departments of Education and Health and Human Services. Falender perceived that this organization had incredible potential influence over several critical issues but "faced many large management challenges." Falender received a job offer at what was then the Office of Education, spending four years in five different jobs in the department. He notes that his MBA training "could not have been more appropriate" because in each position he needed to quickly analyze issues with which he had little prior experience, determine the key issues, set goals, and "use analytic and interpersonal skills to get from here to there." The skills, says Falender, "helped me figure out how to turn potential into reality." Furthermore, after solving problems for the corporate subjects of three cases a day all year in business school, he could now apply the same skills to situations "where I could really make a difference in something I cared about. It kept me motivated."

The next phase of Falender's life brought him to Boston, where he embarked on a networked job search that consisted of "going through every contact I had in the Boston area, until I stumbled into the brother of an officemate in D.C., who was a consultant in Boston, and happened to be doing pro-bono work for the New England Conservatory of Music." As luck would have it, the conservatory was in the midst of reorganization and needed a director of administration and finance. "Finding this opportunity was a matter of timing and luck," he says. Another interesting aspect of Falender's taking the job with the conservatory was that "I am the most nonmusical person you've ever met." But the conservatory was looking for someone to "fix the financial mess and build on its potential," not someone who would try to intervene in the musical aspects of its mission and strategy. Falender fit well and spent fourteen years at the conservatory, ultimately becoming the organization's CEO. "Again, my role was to analyze the organization and its environment, to look at the resources available—from the respect it had earned in the community, to the financial resources, to the people who worked and studied there—and to develop a strategy to enable the organization to grow and prosper."

After fourteen years Falender felt it was time to move on. "The president—who was a musician—was clearly capable of doing both our jobs." Plus, Falender felt that he had achieved what he set out to do when he joined the conservatory, which was to turn around the financial situation, redirect the organization, and put it on a path of dynamic growth. "My next career shift was almost ironic. I had been hiking with my wife in the Dolemites in northern Italy, and can remember looking across the mountain summits and saying to her that if anything could pull me away from the conservatory, it would be the Appalachian Mountain Club." Soon after his return to Boston, Falender discovered that AMC was in fact looking for a new CEO!

The challenges at AMC were similar to those facing Falender at HEW and the conservatory. The organization had a long, strong history and great potential, but faced significant obstacles in financial management, governance, and future direction. "Again, my greatest challenge was to make the most out of the resources available at AMC—to determine where we wanted to go and to make it happen."

The AMC's mission is to promote the protection, enjoyment, and wise use of the mountains, rivers, and trails of the Northeast. The organization has a wide range of programs to achieve that mission, including managing huts in the mountains for overnight visitors; running a chain of retail shops; offering workshops, tours, and educational trips; doing advocacy work on critical issues for the Northeast; developing and selling guidebooks; and more. Falender notes, "Our biggest risk is that we won't accomplish enough with the great assets we have." At the same time, he adds, "the diversity of our activities and our constituents means that focus is absolutely critical if we want to be effective."

Falender's experiences show that finding great jobs in the social sector is very possible but requires extensive networking and relationship development. Still, he recognizes that nonprofits need to do a better job of recruiting talented MBAs. "Our organization survives and thrives on hiring the very best people. We need to think more about how to do just that."

CHAPTER FIVE

Understanding the Subsectors

Overview

This section of the guide discusses a range of fields of interest within the social enterprise area, based on interest expressed by MBA students and alumni. It covers twelve subsectors:

- Arts and culture

- Community economic development

- Community development financial institutions

- Education

- Environment

- Foundations

- Government

- Health care

- International development

- Social services

- Social purpose businesses

- Socially responsible business/community relations

These categories are not meant to be exhaustive, nor are they mutually exclusive. Rather, they are intended to help you learn more about some of the different areas you might choose to focus on through social enterprise careers. Each of the subsector profiles that follows provides an overview of the field and any subcategories within it, current "hot topics," and some thoughts on roles for MBAs. Personal profiles of MBAs working in those fields are interspersed throughout each section.

Arts and Culture

Overview

Arts and culture organizations make up a relatively small part of the nonprofit sector (only about 3 percent of nonprofit organizations, according to The Foundation Center), but play a highly visible and important societal role nonetheless. These organizations gained prominence in the United States during the nineteenth century. Despite much diversity, most included education as part of their mission. While these organizations continue to operate with educational missions today, many sit on the boundary between education and entertainment, competing for funding and audience with both groups. Most organizations are supported by a combination of ticket sales, memberships, gift shop revenues, and charitable donations and grants.

Arts and culture can be subdivided into three main categories: fine arts (museums, galleries, etc.); performing arts (theater, dance, music, etc.); and public radio/TV.

Subdivisions

Fine Arts (Museums and Galleries)
Museums span a wide range of genres including, but not limited to, art, science, history, military, maritime, youth, zoos, and arboretums. Everything from the Metropolitan Museum of Art in New York, to the Rock and Roll Museum in Cleveland, to the San Diego Zoo in California falls into the museum category. Despite this variety, a vast number of the 10,000 museums in the United States are small, historic houses. Only the top 5 percent of museums in this country have operating budgets of $7 million or more. Museums strive to expose a broad population to arts and culture, and to educate this population through such exposure. For example, the Boston Children's Mu-

seum and the Museum of Science are both very involved in education, providing after-school programs for children and enrichment programs for teachers. Art museums often host educational seminars and discussion groups both for museum members and for interested members of the public. However, to draw a broader crowd, museums must also appeal to visitors as a leisure activity.

MBAs considering a career in museums might consider segmenting museums by funding source rather than by content. This distinction is useful for two reasons. First, the most common MBA career path in museums is through the finance department. Second, the structure of funding will determine much of how an executive director spends his or her time. Segmentation by funding sources is as follows:

- *Privately funded.* This model is most common among smaller museums. Executive directors in these museums must spend a large portion of their time fund-raising and considering ways to earn income through gate receipts or store sales.

- *Endowment-funded.* Museums like the Cleveland Museum have traditionally relied on their endowment for a large portion of their income. While this strategy allows flexibility in programming, it may also be subject to market upheavals or unusual investment restrictions. Executive directors of museums funded this way spend a greater portion of their time on investment issues.

- *Government-funded.* The Smithsonian is the best-known example of this type of museum. In addition, the Philadelphia Museum of Art derives a part of its support (land and some support services) from the city of Philadelphia. Reliance on government funding allows more flexibility, but may also suffer under certain political pressures. In fact, the executive director of some of these museums may be a political appointee.

- *University-funded.* Museums associated with educational institutions, like the Yale Art Museum, typically derive their income from the university budget. Association with an educational institution provides access to top-notch scholars, archives, and other university resources. However, these museums do not generally have boards of directors separate from the board for the university, which poses unique management challenges.

Performing Arts
The performing arts include music, dance, theater, and combinations of the three. Within each, there are three distinct categories of organizations: performance groups, performance venues, and distribution channels.

- *Performance groups.* These include symphony orchestras, dance troupes, opera companies, theater companies, and choral groups, among others. In size and scope, the largest organizations tend to be orchestras, followed by opera companies. Many of the largest orchestras have very large management staffs; some of the smaller are run completely by volunteer members of the organization. Well-known performance groups include the Chicago Symphony Orchestra, the Boston Pops, and the New York City Ballet.

- *Performance venues.* Performance halls have also become an important part of the arts sector. Arts complexes like the Kennedy Center in Washington, D.C., the Metropolitan Opera House, and Lincoln Center in New York City house many of the country's largest performing groups. Since groups travel around the country, performance venues have their own management staffs to oversee the various events and performances that occur almost nightly in their halls.

- *Distribution channels.* The distribution area of the arts sector is made up of mostly for-profit organizations, including recording companies, artist management firms, and radio and TV stations. These organizations often play a crucial role in choosing which performing groups and types of music reach larger audiences.

Public Television and Radio Stations
Public TV and radio fall into the distribution channel definition, but can also be defined as a category of their own. Public TV and radio stations play a large role in bringing arts, culture, and education to the general public, often creating their own content (such as WGBH's *Reading Rainbow* programming). Like other arts and culture organizations, public TV and radio face increasing cost pressures given recent funding trends.

Hot Topics

Shifting Financial Landscape. Many arts and culture organizations have faced increasing financial pressures over the last twenty years. Income sources have changed dramatically, forcing arts organizations to decrease reliance on grants (from the National Endowment for the Arts, corporations, and foundations) and to increase reliance on earned income such as ticket sales or shops. Additionally, costs have risen, especially in artist compensation and advertising. Many smaller organizations have faced insolvency, while even the largest organizations have been drawing heavily on their endowments. As a result, many organizations have been forced to develop and pursue more creative funding strategies, including related business/earned-income ventures and unique business partnerships.

Balancing Traditional and New/Cutting-edge Content. Arts organizations often struggle to provide programs that are popular and familiar while still offering unusual or cutting-edge programs. Program directors search for the middle ground—events and exhibits that will draw new crowds without driving away the faithful.

Misappropriation of Cultural Property (mainly museums). High-profile media coverage and legal battles have created a difficult legal, ethical, and political issue for museums regarding true ownership of many items in their collections. Academic research has discovered that some museum collections include art taken from its rightful owners by members of the Nazi organization during World War II, which stirs up controversy over whether (and how) to return the pieces to the rightful owners. In addition, new respect for native peoples and the dead has altered how museums choose to display items as diverse as Native American ceremonial garb and Egyptian mummies.

Reduced Arts Education in Schools. Decreased funding for arts education in schools during the 1980s and 1990s has affected arts organizations in two major ways. First, in an effort to compensate for this loss, arts organizations have extended the breadth of community and childhood arts education and appreciation activities. Motivated in part by mission, this response is also an effort at self-preservation, as arts organizations recognize that childhood arts education is the best predictor of later interest in and support for the arts. Second, as children without arts education have grown to adulthood, the public attending cultural events is less familiar with the arts and less comfortable with art outside the mainstream.

Shifting Organizational Leadership (mainly performing arts). As recently as the 1970s, most large performing arts organizations were identified with a very recognizable musical director, such as George Szell with the Cleveland Orchestra or Sir Georg Solti with the Chicago Symphony. However, as conductors are now able to fly all over the world in search of performance fees and recording opportunities, the role of the music director has changed dramatically. Beyond a few exceptions, performing groups can no longer count on the long-term leadership, community involvement, and marketing image that these leaders used to provide. As a result, executive directors and staff managers are also now called on more

heavily to play a role in artistic decisions and in the overall leadership of the performing group.

Technology (mainly museums). As technology improvements have made digital imaging more realistic, museums and other organizations struggle with how to best use the Internet to effectively expand their reach.

Roles for MBAs

In general, the arts management field has an extremely traditional approach to recruitment and advancement. Candidates are expected to "earn their stripes" through a series of positions across functions and often across organizations. Many positions within these organizations are difficult for an MBA to break into without relevant expertise in the field. For example, an MBA does not prepare you to be a curator, to choreograph the next dance program, or to perform in an orchestra.

MBAs will most likely be welcomed into specific functional areas, such as marketing, strategic planning/business development, or finance, especially in larger organizations. Earned-income operations such as gift shops also provide good opportunities for MBAs to break into the field, especially as cultural organizations increasingly rely on self-generated revenue rather than grants. Larger organizations often present better opportunities because of both their published job openings and their ability to pay for MBAs.

The executive director role is obviously a highly desirable position. MBAs hired to fill this role in an arts and culture organization tend to follow one of two career paths. One path is to take a staff position at a large museum, gain experience and develop relationships in the field, and then move to a senior role in a smaller organization. A less common path is a late career transfer from a more traditional MBA career combined with active volunteer and/or board involvement, to a more senior management position. It is rare to see MBAs (without significant experience in the field) leading arts organizations simply because most do not have the artistic or musical credentials that hiring committees seek. However, some arts organizations, especially larger ones, have recently divided the director role into two jobs—that of executive director with general management responsibility, and that of artistic director with responsibility for programming. This opens the door for greater involvement of MBAs in the senior management team.

For additional resources and addresses of arts and culture organizations, see the Resource Road Map.

JOHN McCARTER

Striving for profits—for different reasons

From his vantage point as president of the Field Museum of Natural History in Chicago, John McCarter (Harvard Business School, MBA 1963), comments: "I think the three sectors are much more similar than dissimilar. Though the substance in which you're dealing is different, you are always thinking about how to create a strategic framework for your decisions, and you always struggle with resource allocation." McCarter has spent time in the corporate, government, and nonprofit sectors. He notes, "We still want 'profits,' we just want them for different reasons—to reinvest in the museum rather than to distribute to shareholders. If you completely lose that for-profit mentality, you won't have money to reinvest in your mission."

Even as an undergraduate, McCarter was attracted to both the business and the public sectors. After graduating from the Woodrow Wilson School at Princeton University in 1960 he went to the London School of Economics, where he enjoyed studying both law and economics. "And then I had to take a class in torts," he recalls, which convinced him to attend HBS rather than law school.

McCarter joined Booz·Allen & Hamilton's Chicago office after business school. After three years he was selected to be a White House Fellow. After a year in D.C., he returned to Booz·Allen and spent most of his time working with public institutions such as hospitals and universities. During that time he got to know Illinois Governor Richard Ogilvie, and in 1969 he became state budget director. "This was a wonderful time of enormous creativity in state government," McCarter comments.

His next move was to DeKalb, an agricultural genetics firm. "At the time, the neo-Malthusian fear of massive shortages was prominent, and we worked hard to build our business." McCarter had responsibility for the seed business (soybeans, corn, etc.), and eventually became president of the company. After thirteen years, a conflict left him jobless, and he was asked to return to the Booz·Allen partnership group. He spent the next ten years working primarily with agricultural, consumer product, and food businesses, and undertook several pro-bono projects with clients that included the Chamber of Commerce, the City of Chicago, and the Chicago Board of Education.

And then "out of the blue," a friend—the chair of the board of the Chicago Field Museum, Leo Mullin (Harvard Business School, MBA 1967 and current CEO of Delta Airlines)—"made me a crazy proposition." But maybe it wasn't so crazy, because on October 1, 1996, John McCarter became president of the Field Museum.

> *"Don't bifurcate the world into for-profit and non-profit. Choose a first job where you will be associated with bright, excited, ambitious people—whichever sector that may be.*

"My first step was to learn about the museum. We have over seventy-two Ph.D.s on staff and a tremendous amount of knowledge." McCarter also undertook a series of "deferred maintenance projects" to rebuild and restore the museum and to invest in its long-term sustainability. The museum opened seven new permanent and traveling exhibits and established a new store, two new restaurants (and two new bathrooms), new benches, signs, a guide and map to the museum ("it's about a million square feet," he says)—about forty-seven projects in all. He also spends a significant amount of time on fund-raising from a wide variety of sources: "foundations; government organizations such as the National Science Foundation, the National Aeronautics Space Administration, the Environmental Protection Agency; the Department of Education; and several corporations, including former consulting clients."

The Field Museum has undertaken several partnerships with public and private organizations. "We are very involved in education and work very closely with the public schools." For example, the museum works with science teachers and organizes activities for inner-city schools. "The nice thing about museums is that you can learn at your own pace." Plus, "children learn in multiple ways, and the museum can tap into that more easily than the traditional classroom structure." McCarter notes that the impact of working with schools is "tremendous."

One of the museum's major undertakings is an exhibit on the Tyrannosaurus Rex using "Sue," a T-Rex fossil bought at an auction. Staff members are now restoring the fossil in a lab in full view (behind a glass wall) of all visitors. "The vertebrae are two feet across," McCarter says, "and people love watching the restoration happen!" The museum is also working with McDonald's, Disney, and other partners on the T-Rex project. They are putting together a traveling exhibit and a curriculum about the T-Rex for use in schools. The material will be sent to 65,000 schools—leveraging the museum's knowledge and curriculum development skills, and McDonald's mailing list, packaging, and financial support.

Many of the museum's other projects are partnerships as well, whether with other museums, corporations (they worked closely with Monsanto Company, ConAgra, the Board of Trade, and the Prince Charitable Trust on an exhibit about biodiversity called "Underground Adventure"), or public entities (much of the educational outreach work is done in partnership with the Department of Education). The key to successful partnerships, according to McCarter, is "a confluence of interest. You have to have enough people who really care about an issue to get the level of involvement you need."

McCarter's path from the corporate world to the nonprofit world is a relatively common one among MBAs currently in social enterprise. He notes: "I learned so much at Booz·Allen, in terms of work habits, how to keep current intellectually, and how to come up with deliverables in a timely fashion." However, he cautions that his is not the only route. "Don't bifurcate the world into for-profit and nonprofit. Choose a first job where you will be associated with bright, excited, ambitious people—whichever sector that may be. This is the pattern you want to establish for a successful and fulfilling career."

PAUL JUDY

Launching a nonprofit to help nonprofits

Paul Judy (Harvard Business School, MBA 1958) began his career in Chicago as a member of the investment securities firm A.G. Becker & Company. He worked there for twenty-three years, eventually retiring in 1981, and then spent ten more years as a professional director of a variety of corporations. During his career at A.G. Becker, he had focused most of his civic activity on the Chicago Symphony Orchestra (CSO). He became a member of the CSO board in 1970, soon after becoming president of A.G. Becker. "While on the board I served in a number of functional areas, including fundraising, corporate development, and the annual fund. Eventually I became part of the executive committee and was elected president of the board in 1980." Judy retired from the CSO board in 1983, soon after his retirement from A.G. Becker.

Nearly ten years later, as Judy was coming to the end of his career as a professional director, the CSO invited him to return to lead its long-range planning process. This new role involved all facets of the orchestra, from the musicians to the staff to the board itself. "I spent a lot of time doing research, including interviewing many individuals from orchestras across the country. I found that the long-range issue facing these organizations was their inability to adapt to their changing environment. Their internal processes were very traditional, very functional, and often based on past mythology."

Soon after the completion of the CSO long-range planning process, Judy again tried to decide whether to retire completely. However, he was interested in continuing the research that he had done with the CSO, and in broadening its scope. So instead of retiring, he launched a nonprofit organization, the Symphony Orchestra Institute (SOI), in 1994. The mission of the institute is to "improve the effectiveness of symphony orchestra organizations, to enhance the value they provide to their communities, and to help assure the preservation of such organizations as unique and valuable cultural institutions." An important focus within this mission is to better utilize the financial and human resources available to orchestras throughout North America.

The Symphony Orchestra Institute began with the creation of *Harmony,* a quarterly magazine dedicated to exploring issues of orchestra leadership and organization. In addition, the SOI has launched three long-term initiatives alongside *Harmony.* The first is to support traditional scholarly research on the organizational charac-

teristics of arts organizations. The second is to obtain membership support from a broad base of symphony orchestras. Judy's goal for this effort was to sign up 100 orchestras in five years; one year later, over 100 had already joined. The third initiative is to develop models of organizational change by observing changes in large symphony orchestras. Examples include reporting on an innovative musicians' contract in Kansas City and a long-range planning process in Pittsburgh.

Though the SOI is only three and a half years old, Judy feels that it has already gained quite a bit of credibility within the orchestra field. The organization and its membership continue to grow, and Judy has begun to think about finding a successor. He has "failed" at retiring twice before, but is pretty sure that the third time will be successful.

Community Economic Development

Overview

Community economic development (CED) facilitates economic growth in urban and rural areas characterized by slow or nonexistent economic growth and concentrated poverty. CED is distinct from the broader category of economic development in that it refers to economic development within the United States (international development is covered in a separate section later in this chapter). Although CED involves significant housing development work, it is distinct from homelessness and homeless shelters, which fall into the social service category.

The primary organizations involved in CED are the government and community development corporations (CDCs), although religious institutions and job-training organizations have become significantly more active in the field. In its early stages, CED primarily emphasized building and maintaining affordable housing. As the field has grown and evolved, emphasis has shifted from housing alone to the holistic improvement of communities. Progressive CDCs now:

- focus on activities that are broader than "bricks and mortar";

- emphasize community organizing as a strategy for identifying the needs of a specific community;

- help develop community building plans, rather than building without regard to larger urban plans;

- include and involve neighborhood residents in changes;

- create clear accountability between the CDC and the community; and

- develop collaborative relationships with other CDCs.

CDCs are nonprofit organizations that work at the grass-roots level in communities to increase affordable housing, employ workers, and provide child care or education. They are primarily funded through financial intermediaries, including local financial institutions, foundations, and government tax credits and grants. Community development financial institutions (CDFIs), a specific group of funders focused almost exclusively on economic development organizations, are described in detail in the next section.

The CDC field is highly fragmented, largely due to the grass-roots nature of the need. The National Conference on Community Economic Development estimates there are approximately 2,000 CDCs nationwide. CDCs work closely with community groups, churches and other religious institutions, and local and national government to ensure that they are meeting the needs of the community they serve.

CDCs typically use one of two development strategies. "People-based" strategies focus on improving the economic status of a particular population (for example, African-Americans on Chicago's North Side) regardless of where that economic development may take place. In this example, a people-based CDC would likely seek out employment opportunities throughout Chicago and then work to transport the African-American population to places where living-wage jobs can be found.

"Place-based" strategies work to develop a particular area, regardless of the population that moves in or out (for example, the Lower East Side of Manhattan). In this case, the CDC would work to develop affordable housing, services, and community resources on the Lower East Side, regardless of the fact that the population in this area is constantly changing with new waves of immigration and shifts in economic conditions.

Subdivisions

Housing Development
Housing development is exactly what it sounds like: building and maintaining (developing) affordable housing for low- to middle-income families who would otherwise be left with no place to live or forced to live in unacceptable conditions. Housing development can be public or private. Public housing development takes place through the Department of Housing and Urban Development (HUD) and local housing authorities. Private housing development is facilitated by both for-profit and nonprofit organizations.

The U.S. government did not become involved in housing development until the dire economics of the Great Depression forced President Franklin D. Roosevelt to support subsidized housing in 1937. Interestingly enough, the primary beneficiaries of this program were middle-class homeowners, not the poor or disadvantaged. During the 1960s, Congress enacted a series of urban initiatives that included public housing programs. These programs were set up to foster public-private partnerships whereby public subsidies were given to for-profit developers. This model had serious execution problems because developers had mixed incentives, and critics claimed that clustering low-income housing simply created "vertical ghettos" rather than eradicating the sources of national poverty.

Finally, in 1974, President Richard Nixon authorized a new system of tenant-based rental certificates and vouchers—the Section 8 program. The program had two parts. The first essentially provided households with the difference between what they could afford (estimated at 25 to 30 percent of household income) and the Fair Market Rent (FMR) for an apartment in their area. The second

continued the project subsidy approach of the past but with stronger control mechanisms. The mission of most CDCs makes them likely purchasers of Section 8 housing projects, as does their experience in managing multifamily homes in many downtrodden areas.

Although this project subsidy program was phased out in 1983, it successfully produced one million units of housing, and the voucher program continues to provide rental assistance to approximately 1.5 million households. However, the "Reagan Revolution" of the 1980s saw a drastic slashing of the Department of Housing and Urban Development budget—from a peak of $32.2 billion in 1978 to only $9.8 billion in 1988, an inflation-adjusted decline of more than 80 percent. Under President Bill Clinton, federal support for housing remained insufficient. In 1995, no new Section 8 vouchers were made available—at a time when the demand for low-income housing was at its highest ever.

Section 8 Legislation. Section 8 has three sets of provisions. One provision is project-based and provides subsidies (mostly to for-profit developers) for construction and rehabilitation of units designated for low-income households and for long-term rental subsidies. The program has helped create over 1.7 million affordable apartments.

A second provision created a certificate program through which HUD provides certificates to public housing authorities (PHAs), who then distribute them to qualified tenants. The tenants pay 30 percent of their household income to the landlords, and the PHAs pay the difference between that amount and the amount HUD determined to be the FMR for that area. The landlords have to agree to accept only FMR.

The third provision—the voucher program—is similar to the certificate program, but tenants receive vouchers to pay for housing that may be more expensive than FMR. However, tenants are responsible for any amount of rent still due after they have paid the 30 percent of their household income and the PHAs have paid the difference between that and the FMR.

Title VI Legislation. The Low Income Housing Preservation and Resident Homeownership Act (Title VI) was enacted by Congress in 1992 as part of the National Affordable Housing Act. Title VI intended to keep owners of older, assisted housing from buying out of subsidized mortgages and thereby reducing the number of available affordable housing units. The act is meant to encourage property owners to remain in HUD programs and to allow tenants and nonprofits first right of refusal if the property owner ultimately decides to sell.

Workforce Development

Workforce development refers to job training and placement activities that help poor individuals gain jobs and economic independence. Several factors have contributed to a tremendous increase in the field of workforce development in the last several years. Unemployment rates in many cities have dipped below 6 percent (considered "full employment" by economists), while labor markets have become tighter in many ex-urban and suburban areas. As a result, companies are having greater difficulty filling lower-level, lower-paying jobs. At the same time, the "Personal Responsibility and Work Opportunity Reconciliation Act of 1996" ended the sixty-one-year guarantee that the government would provide welfare checks to all eligible low-income mothers and children.

In this era of welfare reform, the task of helping disadvantaged people enter or reenter the labor market has become more urgent than ever. Welfare recipients have moved off the welfare rolls in unprecedented numbers, creating an entire work area dedicated to the successful migration from welfare to work of individuals who have had long absences from the working world. Most experts agree that job training and employment services have had a mixed track record, but innovative and successful programs are out there looking for talent to help them meet this national challenge.

Nonprofit organizations have played a tremendous role in workforce development. They frequently act as intermediaries to provide training, job screening, vocational counseling, and child care to individuals reentering the work force. Some examples include Jobs for the Future (Boston), Bidwell Training Center (Pittsburgh), STRIVE, and other programs. For-profit social enterprises such as WorkSource Staffing Partnership Inc. (see profile later in this chapter) have also become involved in welfare-to-work initiatives. In addition, community organizations often work to ensure that former welfare recipients have adequate transportation from their homes to their places of employment. Many companies choose to partner with nonprofit organizations, who then act as their "screeners" to assess job applicants, conduct initial training, and help smooth the transition to the workplace.

Workforce development programs cater to many different populations. Some focus on welfare recipients, some on people with disabilities, and others on displaced workers who need retraining. Program offerings may consist of one or more of the following:

- *"Soft skills" training* teaches good work habits to participants, such as arriving to work on time, getting along well with co-workers, calling in when they have to miss work, etc.

- *"Hard skills" training* teaches specific job skills, such as word processing or cooking, to prepare clients for an entry-level job.

- *Job readiness* workshops help participants prepare resumes and learn interview skills to prepare for the job search process.

- *Job clubs* gather groups of participants together, usually with a facilitator, to support one another as they go through the job-search process. They may help review each other's resumes or help each other with practice interviews.

- *Job developers* are staff members that "market" the program to employers and try to generate job leads to participants. They will sometimes act as brokers in the interview process, setting up interviews for clients and following up with the employer to see if he or she was satisfied with the candidates interviewed.

- *Transportation and child care assistance.* Many welfare recipients, especially in isolated, low-income urban areas, find that jobs are inaccessible without transportation assistance. Women with children need someone to take care of their children while they work. As a result, some job-training agencies have begun to help their clients connect with child care and transportation resources.

- *Follow-up.* Many agencies are becoming increasingly concerned with follow-up and re-placement services. Studies indicate that long-term unemployed people often go through a series of jobs before settling into stable career paths. Some program directors argue that programs need to follow up on job placements to help keep people in jobs and to develop the capacity to place people into second and third jobs. Even after a person has been successful in a job, he or she may desire additional training and assistance moving up a career ladder.

Hot Topics

Creating Sustainable Communities. CDCs are increasingly recognizing the need for a long-term, market-based approach to economic development. Many have extended their efforts beyond housing to include education, child care, workforce development, and other activities to strengthen entire communities rather than focusing on one specific element. The Community Builders Inc. (see profile of Ted Preston in chapter 2), is a prime example of this holistic approach to building stronger, sustainable communities.

CDC Involvement in Revenue-Generating Activities. In recent years, a number of other types of organizations have evolved to complement the more traditional CDCs. Many of these organizations run businesses that provide training opportunities for people in the community and generate revenue for the organization. Revenue-generating activities are fairly controversial for some CDCs; tread lightly when discussing these issues before you discern an organization's particular emphasis.

Declining Government Support for Section 8 Housing Efforts. Continued funding for the Section 8 program remained hotly contested in 1998, while the question of who owns homes with expiring Section 8 contracts loomed as well. While government support of housing development continues to shrink, for-profit institutions and hybrid solutions like vouchers have become the dominant alternatives.

Mixed-Income Neighborhoods and Wealth Creation through Home Ownership. There is strong support in the field for additional emphasis on government incentives for the development of housing that will be sold to low- and middle-income families, rather than rented, to create a sense of community ownership and empowerment. At the same time, there is a shift from low-income projects composed of impersonal skyscrapers to mixed-income neighborhoods developed as more personal and integrated townhouse communities.

The Importance of "Soft/Attitudinal Skills" in Workforce Development Programs. Successful job-training models have found that the "softer life and attitudinal skills" are critical to success in the workplace, especially for poor, inner-city welfare recipients who have not been exposed to corporate culture and expectations.

The Need for Corporate Partnerships in Workforce Development. In addition to attitudinal training, workforce development programs need to partner with employers to train people for specific job skills, with clear post-training opportunities at those partnering employers.

Bidwell Services and JFY/Boston have both been successful with such partnerships.

Roles for MBAs

Individuals who work for community development corporations traditionally come from a policy, government, or local community background, but a growing number of MBAs are entering the field as executive directors and financial officers in these organizations. The environment is often highly entrepreneurial, unstructured, and diverse. Many CDCs are small organizations (one to ten people), and they marshal resources from outside their direct control. Often a CDC has one executive director (ED), one development (fund-raising) director full- or part-time, and several community organizers. CDCs sometimes also employ one or more "analysts" who evaluate real estate deals, manage the money of the organization, and determine where financial resources should be allocated with the direction of the ED. MBAs, especially those with real estate and financial services experience, are highly valued in housing development. It is very common to find individuals who have made a career shift from real estate development or banking (for-profit) to nonprofit work, since the skills are so readily applicable.

MBAs in the *workforce development* field often work with local and state governments to set up and administer comprehensive training programs on behalf of nonprofit organizations. In addition, some MBAs work in the human resources departments of corporations to create successful welfare-to-work strategies to incorporate new workers into the organization. Finally, some nonprofits employ policy analysts or MBAs to assess the workforce needs within a regional area so that new training programs can be developed to meet the needs of for-profit employers. These "job developers" often serve a vocational counseling role as well for a specific group of new employees.

MBAs looking for summer internship opportunities in CED will do well to consider Students for Responsible Business (NetImpact) internships, since CED is one of the "internship tracks." Because the program provides significant structure and training for the internship, the high-impact experience is very effective.

For additional resources and addresses of community economic development organizations, see the Resource Road Map.

NEIL SILVERSTON

Developing a motivated workforce

Neil Silverston (Harvard Business School, MBA 1987) has moved in and out of the social enterprise sector. "Immediately after business school, I worked with a group of others to start City Year. After a couple years working on that start-up, I then spent four years in consulting. By 1994, however, I wanted to get back into entrepreneurial public service. I spent 1994 and 1995 talking to people about temporary employment services as a vehicle for welfare to work, and focused on putting together a business plan. In November 1995, we rolled out Worksource Staffing Partnership Inc."

WorkSource Staffing, which serves the greater Boston and central Massachusetts areas, "helps tap the enormous potential in our communities to develop a more loyal, motivated workforce." Among its activities are community outreach, ongoing mentoring support, and individual career development. As president of this for-profit social enterprise, Silverston's responsibilities are numerous. "I do everything from the actual staffing that we do, to support activities like recruiting, marketing, and finance. My MBA learning has been invaluable in this role."

Looking back on his work, Silverston points to his original experience with City Year as defining. "City Year was really a mission-driven *company*. The time I spent there empowered me to use the skills that I had gained at business school to make a positive difference in people's lives, while helping me to build the foundation for the person I am today. The experience allowed me to get broad, hands-on business experience in a short time after finishing business school. These skills have been relevant throughout my business experiences." But Silverston also mentions one of the challenges of pursu-

ing a nonprofit job immediately after graduating: "There was also probably no one who made less money right out of school."

Keeping this in mind, Silverston offers the following recommendations to students interested in a career in social enterprise. "There are two schools of thought: you can make money early on and get into social enterprise work when you have the flexibility, or you can go directly into it after graduation. I would encourage you to consider this: if you believe you have the ability to change the world, go for it now!

"And don't think of it as taking time out from your career. The nonprofit world is *not* an entirely different realm from business. In addition to your ability to bring significant skills to the table, you will also have the chance to gain pure business

> *"If you believe you have the ability to change the world, go for it now!"*

experience. The execution, marketing, and financial skills that are so important in for-profit business are equally important in nonprofits. In addition, a job in the social enterprise sector embraces a generalist approach and encourages the development of the personal skills required of a general manager."

So what does he look for in potential hires? "I look for someone who has business skills *and* is driven by our social purpose. The business skills are key because we need someone who can help us build the company, market the organization, and really help take us to the next level. However, it's equally important that the person is mission-driven. He or she should able to recognize that our mission of tapping into community potential *is* the business opportunity."

ARIEL ZWANG

Bringing banking skills to combat urban poverty

Ariel Zwang (Harvard Business School, MBA 1990) worked in investment banking before she came to business school and in management consulting after graduation. However, after a year at the Boston Consulting Group (BCG, a management consulting firm), Zwang realized that she wanted to do something different. "Consulting didn't do it. I didn't want to look back fifty years later to see that all I did was to help my clients increase their market share by 7 percent." With the help of career seminars sponsored by the HBS Alumni Club of New York, Zwang spent a full year trying to figure out what she wanted. She identified her strong interest in urban poverty and found a job as the special assistant to the chancellor of the New York City Schools.

"In one of the career workshops, we were asked what our greatest obstacle to finding our ideal job/career was. I said it was connections. The HBS Club representative then suggested a contact to whom I sent my resume. This person passed my resume to a friend at the Citibank Foundation, who passed it on to someone else, who passed it on to a member of the board of education, which ultimately led to my getting the position of special assistant." Three years later, Zwang went through a similar networking process to discover the Women's Housing and Economic Development Corporation (WHEDCO), where she is currently the vice president of operations.

Located in the South Bronx, WHEDCO was founded by an ex-legal aid attorney to support the economic empowerment of low-income women. By embracing a holistic program that includes housing, job training, counseling, and health care, WHEDCO helps women "move from welfare dependency to independence." In addition to managing 132 units of low-income housing and providing counseling services, WHEDCO runs a family child care program (that recently received Head Start funding), a commercial kitchen (retail food preparation, catering, and wholesale baking), a fitness center, and other vocational training programs.

Zwang cites the challenges of managing an organization with a "double bottom line"—one of both financial and social return. "Bad management is rampant. Finding people with knowledge of spreadsheets and accounting is also tough—some people were treating revenues as profits. But overall, working for WHEDCO has been very much like working for any start-up. In the past three years, we have grown from eight employees to forty-five. Although we have a six-person board, it is still very much in the image of the founder."

When asked how she allocates her time on a typical day, Zwang answers that it would roughly be 25 percent on oversight of the commercial kitchen and fitness center, 25 percent on internal planning, and the remaining 50 percent on overall administrative issues. Zwang also points out that WHEDCO has been very "family friendly," allowing her to work at home with flexible hours that enable her to spend more time with her young daughter. However, she admits that as WHEDCO grows, this flexibility may decline a bit.

> *"Spend your second year talking to as many people as will talk to you and find out what they do and what they like about it."*

What advice does she have for business school students? "First, leverage your informal networks! Spend your second year talking to as many people as will talk to you and find out what they do and what they like about it. Both of my social enterprise jobs were the result of this informal networking, not organized recruiting. Second, general preparation is the best preparation. You don't need to know *everything* about finance or marketing."

Weighing the question of whether to go straight into social enterprise or to follow a path more like her own, Zwang says that working in the for-profit sector first was good for her. "Not only did it allow me to command a higher salary than I could have had in a nonprofit right away, working at BCG also demonstrated that I had strong practical experience, not just an education. It had credential value that worked as a signal." However, she cautions that not everyone in the nonprofit sector will value such experience. Some still adhere to the notion that nonprofits should be run by former social workers rather than MBAs.

Community Development Financial Institutions (CDFIs)

Overview

CDFIs are private sector, financial intermediaries with community development as their primary mission. They can be either for-profit or nonprofit in structure, though many are nonprofit. They strive to rebuild distressed and neglected communities through a mix of lending, investment, and other support, usually by finding ways to get funds to "unconventional borrowers" that traditional financial institutions would consider "unbankable."

The types of CDFIs vary primarily according to mission, capital sources, customers/borrowers, and financial products and services offered. The five major categories, defined by the CDFI Coalition, are outlined below.

Subdivisions

Community Development Loan Funds (CDLFs)
CDLFs aggregate capital from individual and institutional social investors at below-market rates and re-lend the money primarily to nonprofit housing and business developers in urban and rural lower-income communities. Their varied capital sources include foundations, banks, religious organizations, corporations, government, insurance companies, and individuals. Their borrowers are primarily nonprofit community organizations, social service provider facilities, and small businesses. They offer loans and provide extensive technical assistance before, during, and after the loan transaction. CDLFs are generally nonprofit organizations. Examples include Boston Community Capital and the Low Income Housing Fund.

Community Development Venture Capital Funds (CDVCFs)
CDVCFs provide equity and debt-with-equity products to community organizations and private businesses, primarily to spur economic development and job creation in distressed rural and inner-city areas. They can be for-profit or nonprofit. Their portfolio companies are generally small businesses in distressed communities, and their capital sources include foundations, corporations, individuals, and government. Examples of CDVCFs include the Roberts Enterprise Development Fund and the New York City Investment Fund (launched by Henry Kravis and Jerry Speyer in 1996).

Community Development Credit Unions (CDCUs)
CDCUs promote community ownership of assets and savings and provide affordable credit and retail financial services to lower-income people with special outreach to minority communities. Their borrowers are members of the credit union, and their capital sources include member deposits and nonmember deposits from social investors or government. In addition to consumer banking services, CDCUs provide credit counseling and business planning assistance. Leading CDCUs include the SelfHelp Credit Union in Durham, North Carolina; the Union Settlement FCU in East Harlem, New York; and the Santa Cruz Community Credit Union in California.

Microenterprise Development Institutions (MDIs)
MDIs foster social and business development through loans and technical assistance to low-income people involved in very small businesses, or to self-employed people unable to access conventional credit. Generally nonprofit, MDIs serve low-income entrepreneurs and access capital from foundations and government. They offer start-up and expansion funding as well as training and technical assistance. One such organization is the Center for Women & Enterprise (see profile of Andrea Silbert, chapter 2).

Community Development Banks (CDBs)
CDBs provide capital to rebuild lower-income communities through targeted lending and investment. They tend to be much larger than other organizations and are for-profit corporations, regulated by the Federal Deposit Insurance Corporation (FDIC), the Federal Reserve, and state and local banking agencies. They lend to nonprofit community organizations, individual entrepreneurs, small businesses, and housing developers, while their capital sources are deposits (often below-market investments) from individuals, institutions, and government. South Shore Bank and the Pennsylvania Community Development Bank are leading examples.

Hot Topics

Community Reinvestment Act (CRA). The CRA regulation requires banks to participate in community development activities, including lending, investment, and financial services-related activities, either through direct offerings or through partnership with a CDFI in their area.

Impact of Recent Bank Mergers. As banks across the nation actively strive to gain regulatory approval to merge into "megabanks," a large pool of capital has become available for community development initiatives (for example, through expanded CRA requirements), which creates both opportunities and challenges for CDFIs. There is great opportunity for CDFIs to manage the megabanks' community investments, but there will be a capacity challenge as well as a demand-generation challenge.

Raising Capital/Showing Social Return to Investors. Because CDFIs are investing money for individuals and institutions, they need to somehow demonstrate a return on that investment. However, unlike traditional financial institutions, the most significant measure of return may not be purely financial. This poses a measurement challenge that has yet to be solved. CDFIs struggle to define social return and to measure success. The issue becomes particularly complex because it is very difficult (if not impossible) to establish causal links between community development financing and social outcomes.

Fund Specialization. Just as mutual funds and other mainstream financial products have become increasingly specialized, social funds have begun to focus on subsets of community development as well. Many traditional CDFIs were housing-based, but others have emerged focusing on child care, community health, minority entrepreneurs, and other niches.

Roles for MBAs

In some respects, CDFIs have closely modeled themselves after for-profit financial institutions. Though the social mission of CDFI work is very different than the mission of commercial banks, and the scale is often much smaller, in many respects the required skills and activities are quite similar. MBAs, especially those with financial services experience, are highly valued in the field. It is a very common place to find individuals who have made a career shift from banking (for-profit) to nonprofit work. The banking skills are readily applicable, and yet the job combines aspects of financial and social return.

For additional resources and addresses of CDFI organizations, see the Resource Road Map.

MATT LeBARON

Investing in the inner city

Matt LeBaron (Harvard Business School, MBA 1999) spent the summer of 1998 helping launch Inner City Ventures LLC (ICV), a private equity fund that will target businesses in America's inner cities. ICV is a for-profit affiliate of the Initiative for a Competitive Inner City (ICIC), a national nonprofit organization founded by HBS Professor Michael E. Porter. ICIC's mission is to transform thinking, reinvigorate market forces, and engage the private sector in fostering healthy economies in America's inner cities. The venture fund was a joint undertaking between ICIC and American Securities Capital Partners, LP (ASCP), an established private-equity group based in New York City.

What makes ICV different from ASCP and other private-equity firms? The fund's mission is to spur economic growth in inner cities while generating strong returns for its investors (the fund seeks an internal rate of return of over 30 percent). Additionally, since ICIC owns a piece of the fund, the fund's profits will provide revenue for ICIC. But "understanding the true philosophy is important," says LeBaron. "We invest in the inner city not out of philanthropic impulse, but because we believe that there is untapped opportunity. Though we believe that investing in growing businesses in inner cities will contribute to the revitalization of these communities, the goal of ICV is strictly profit. ICV's goals are in line with ICIC's major premise that inner cities have inherent competitive advantages and untapped market potential—including strategic locations near downtown areas, underserved consumers, and an underutilized work force. We believe that successful businesses can be built or grown by capitalizing on those advantages."

Having worked at Bain Capital prior to business school, LeBaron found that ICV offered a unique opportunity to take on very high levels of responsibility. "I did three main things this summer. First, I helped to structure the fund itself, including the strategic choice of the for-profit legal form, the choice of investors, and other structural decisions. Second, I helped begin the hiring process for the organization. Third—and this was where I spent the majority of my time—I actively sought out investment opportunities, sourcing and assessing potential deals for ICV. It was an amazing experience to do all this on my own. You don't get that kind of responsibility in an established organization."

Though ICV will be a for-profit fund with the goal of generating financial returns for investors, it does differ from traditional firms in many ways. "It was harder to find staff for ICV because of the need for both relevant investment experience and an understanding of and interest in the inner city. We were certainly more committed to diversity than a typical private equity firm." In terms of investing decisions, "we are looking at a very focused market—the inner city. We have to be able to understand that market extremely well in order to assess the viability of deals. And because few other firms have any understanding of the distinct assets (and liabilities) of the inner city as a business location, we encounter much less competition. For example, we put together a bid for a retail chain that sold apparel to inner-city customers, primarily Black and Hispanic women. It was a sizeable company, and an attractive deal, yet there were few other bidders. If a

"ICV's goals are in line with ICIC's major premise that inner cities have inherent competitive advantages and untapped market potential."

deal such as this were in the suburbs, there would have been 100 people on it."

At the same time, ICV has its own set of unique struggles. For example, LeBaron notes, "There is ongoing tension about what an inner-city investment really is. Does the business have to be located in the inner city? Does it have to be a grass-roots enterprise? What if it hires or serves inner-city residents, but operates outside the city? We define inner-city businesses as ones that serve, operate in, hire from, seek to expand into, or are owned by residents of America's inner cities. Inner cities are defined as urban areas with low to moderate income levels (generally more than 20 percent below the metropolitan area average for each inner city). We keep the definition broad because we want to fulfill our mission to improve lives in the inner city, but we don't want to limit our investment options too much or we'll risk generating subpar returns."

In addition to the obvious reason to do deals (to make money), ICV's success with inner-city venture capital investments will lend credibility to ICIC's and ICV's core belief in the competitive advantages and growth potential of inner cities.

DEBORAH WRIGHT

Empowerment through investment

Deborah Wright (Harvard Business School, MBA 1984) is the president and CEO of the Upper Manhattan Empowerment Zone (UMEZ), a $250 million investment fund whose mission is to spur economic and business development in Upper Manhattan. UMEZ is a private institution that receives its financing through matching grants from the city, state, and federal governments. To prepare the inner-city community to enter the mainstream economy, Wright explains, she must translate between two worlds that "do not communicate. . . .

Uptown has been cut off from mainstream financing and technical skills for many decades, and Downtown does not understand the factors that have led to this disinvestment."

Wright believes that both her MBA training and her private sector experience have been invaluable. As she states, "There is no question that I would never have been able to talk to both camps unless I had spent time in each." In addition, these experiences have allowed her to demand higher expectations of the community. As a recent *New York Times* article stated, Wright "is not . . . another traditional social reformer or a politician handing out favors to friends, but a financier who says she holds Harlem to the standards of Wall Street."

Wright's combination of private and public sector experience was not entirely intentional. Upon graduating from Harvard with a joint law and business degree, Wright says she "fell right into the investment banking herd" and joined First Boston as an associate. She soon realized, however, that investment banking was neither suitable to her talents nor personally fulfilling. So Wright left First Boston and took three months to do some soul-searching and explore her options. Her only goal was "to find a job where I wanted to wake up and go to work in the morning."

Eventually, Wright found Ellen Strauss and Kathryn Wylde of the New York City Partnership, a prominent business and civic organization. Wright accepted a job working under Wylde in the housing division, a career change that caused her income to plunge from $135,000 to $35,000. Even so, Wright calls this first year "one of the best years of my life. I felt I was doing something that mattered to people I could touch." She saw that her business skills were vitally important to the organization, and she loved working with her colleagues.

While at the NYC Partnership, Wright developed an expertise in housing. A few years later, Mayor David Dinkins appointed Wright to the City Planning Commission, and then to the New York City Housing Board. When Rudolph Giuliani won the mayoral election in 1994, Wright stayed on as commissioner of the Department of Housing Preservation and Development. In 1996, Congressman Charles Rangel asked Wright to become president and CEO of UMEZ. Initially, Wright refused the position. "After being on the firing lines in government for six straight years, I was ready to make the transition to the private side. I was tired, and I knew the Empowerment Zone would require a 200 percent commitment."

However, a tragic incident in December 1995—shooting deaths at Freddy's Fashion Mart on 125th Street in Harlem—changed her mind. Wright was asked to accompany Mayor Giuliani to meet with local business leaders in Harlem after the incident. Wright recalls, "I took the subway that morning and walked the five blocks from east to west [across 125th Street] and it became obvious that everything I had done in my career had led to this moment."

On her walk she saw "three to four solid blocks of abandoned commercial frontage. Meanwhile, at Freddy's, people had died over 1,000 square feet of real estate." Wright perceived that Harlem's entrepreneurs had no resources to help them develop feasible business strategies, and this lack of infrastructure contributed to a feeling of helplessness, which in this case erupted into violence. She also believed she could change the situation. When she received the second call, this time from Dick Parsons, chair of UMEZ and president of Time Warner Inc., she accepted the job.

"We need people who can communicate between the two worlds [public and private] in order to come to solutions."

Wright's fondest wish is that more people would spend time on either side of the fence [between the public and private spheres], "because we need people who can communicate between the two worlds in order to come to solutions." Her greatest satisfaction comes from changing the expectations of both mainstream business leaders and the community. Marketers who previously thought growth opportunities only existed in the suburbs have come to view Harlem in a whole new light.

Her most important piece of advice to MBA students and alumni is to "find out what fundamentally motivates you." Wright realized that she wanted to change people's lives. As a preacher's daughter and the niece of a famous social activist, Wright recognizes that "public service is the family's business." She says, "I had to get in sync with what I was meant to do." Wright adds, "I do believe fate also has a lot to do with it. But they don't teach you about that at business school."

Education

Overview

The complex and multifaceted education industry spans private, public, and nonprofit organizations and serves people from infancy to retirement. Segmented by age group, the industry comprises the following markets: early childhood; K–12; and higher education. From a product/service perspective, the industry includes basic schooling and instruction, supplemental education and out-of-school programs, textbooks and instructional materials, software and educational toys, tours and trips, and more. Over the past decade, Wall Street has taken more interest in the education industry, and estimates that it ranges from $600 to $800 billion per year in size, $60 to $70 billion of which comes from revenues in the for-profit sector.

Though education has been traditionally a public sector domain, there has been a trend toward decentralization and privatization in the K–12 arena, the largest subdivision of the education industry. Many draw comparisons to what took place in health care in the 1970s and 1980s. This trend has been driven by dissatisfaction with public school performance, which many believe can be improved with more competition, organizational management skills, and avoidance of public sector bureaucracy. With this trend, many business school graduates have become interested in working in the field of education.

Subdivisions

There are several important subdivisions of education, as well as related fields such as educational software and out-of-school enrichment programs:

Early Childhood Education

Child care is increasingly characterized as the first phase of the educational system. Traditionally seen as a social service, child development research and other trends have focused attention on the educational aspects of child care and the critical link between quality care and later development and educational performance. Child care providers can be nonprofit, public, or private, for-profit, and may be independent or part of larger chains. Providers, particularly in the nonprofit sector, are highly fragmented, and most operate a small number of centers within a small region. Many churches and other religious organizations also offer child-care programs. For-profit providers are often large, national chains.

K–12

In the United States, education is mandatory through age sixteen. Within this broad age group are several different kinds of schools, including public, private, and independent or charter schools, described below.

- *Traditional public schools.* Public schools are the most common form of K–12 education in the United States, and are characterized by their funding source—the government. Because they are publicly funded, however, they are subject to strong government regulation. Extensive union contracting makes it difficult for a noncertified individual to find a job in either teaching or administration in the public schools.

- *Private schools.* This group includes independent and parochial schools. Private schools charge tuition, thereby segmenting the K–12 education market along income lines. These schools, although required to meet certain national accreditation standards, are free from unions and government regulation.

- *Charter schools.* Charter schools are a subset of public schools in that they are publicly funded and subject to regulations by the state (which provides the charter). However, they are free from typical public school restrictions such as union contracting and state-mandated curricula. Charter schools are one attempt to achieve greater educational innovation, parent and student choice, and integration of decentralized management tools into education. Since charters only last for five years, charter schools have greater accountability pressures to prove performance if they want to continue to operate.

Higher Education

Higher education includes college, graduate and professional programs, and executive education. Higher education administration and executive education programs at universities and professional schools offer more and more opportunities for business school graduates in admissions, community relations, financial aid, career placement, operations, and program management and development.

Other Education-Related Fields

- *Before-school, after-school, and summer programs.* In addition to basic K–12 education during school hours, "out of school time" has become a concern for parents, teachers, and others. Many organizations have begun offering programs to serve children before and after regular school hours as well as during the summer. Some are academic, others extracurricular. One example of a nonprofit out-of-school program is Citizen Schools, which runs after-school and summer programs for children aged nine to fourteen in which community citizens volunteer to "share a passion" with students.

- *Supplemental education.* In addition to the more community-based out-of-school programs, several organizations (often private, for-profit) provide supplemental education (for example, test preparation, enrichment programs) to the private market and/or public schools. Major providers include Kaplan, well known for its test-preparation products and classes, and Sylvan Learning Centers, which offers remedial math and science tutorial programs for schoolchildren. Another example is EF Education, which offers international tours and exchange programs primarily to middle school and high school students.

- *For-profit school management companies.* Companies such as the Edison Project and Education Alternatives contract with school systems to manage schools, claiming that they can improve quality of education while spending less than the existing public school management.

- *Educational software.* Technology—a fundamental part of our economy and work-life—brings opportunities for training to all levels of students (at home, through formal schooling, and in the workplace). Sometimes called "edutainment," educational software is designed to capture students' interest while helping develop their academic skills. Most companies are for-profit but may have a dual mission. Prominent educational software companies include Broderbund, Computer Curriculum Corporation, and Knowledge Universe.

- *Educational toys.* The Learning Company and Wild Planet Toys, both San Francisco–based companies, are capturing the corner of the market that is trying to bring a standard of quality in purpose, message, material, and educational reinforcement of children's toys. Again, many of these companies fall into the for-profit sector.

- *Corporate training.* A close cousin of executive education, corporate training is a large component of many corporations or consulting firms' human resources budgets. It is used to develop the skills and knowledge of their employees. Developing and managing those training programs present other job opportunities for people interested in the human resources side of companies. This segment tends to include for-profit (and highly profitable) businesses. Prominent firms include Forum

Corporation in Massachusetts and the Center for Creative Leadership in Colorado.

Hot Topics

Privatization and the Rise of Education Management Companies. Increasingly, public schools and systems are contracting with private companies that offer everything from specific curricula to management of an entire school system. Private management companies such as the Edison Project, Beacon Management, and Advantage Schools contract with traditional public schools and charter schools to take over the management of the school, and are accountable to the school board or the charter holder. These companies arose because of the demand for management skills combined with claims that business practices can improve the cost and outcomes of public education.

Integrating Technology. While all schools recognize the importance of technology, many are still figuring out exactly how to incorporate the computer into the teaching day. Many schools have a computer lab and offer computers as a class, and some are also beginning to use the computer as a tool to enhance many different classes. In addition, administrators are glimpsing the possibilities of using more sophisticated software to streamline tasks and to track student information more easily.

Standards. Initially part of the Bush Administration's vision for improving public schools, standards are a typical part of the conservative reform agenda. The idea of standards is simply to lay out exactly what students should be learning in school. While this sounds straightforward, "imposing" such rules from the top is problematic in education, which traditionally has been seen as a local business. At this point, many states are adopting their own standards, but advocates of national standards still face a major battle.

Expanding Role of Schools and Teachers in the Community. While education is a necessary component of developing productive and responsible U.S. citizens, schooling alone is not sufficient. A student's family, neighborhood, health status, and countless other factors also play a huge role in determining a child's future. Schools, realizing that they will continue to be blamed for things that they cannot control, have tried finding ways to work more closely with community organizations to address students' basic and extracurricular needs.

Public–Private Partnerships for Educational Reform. Since the 1980s, the business sector has become more involved in financing and directing school reform. Depending on the city, one can find business councils involved in creating reform plans for the school system, consulting firms advising superintendents on organizational strategy, and businesses "partnering" with individual schools to provide free products, services, management advice, or volunteer time. IBM and Bell Atlantic are two examples of corporations that have become active partners with public school systems.

Roles for MBAs

MBAs interested in education face three distinct job markets: the K–12 system, dominated by public schools; higher education; and the large, private market that sells products and services to both schools and families, which operates in many ways like other consumer products industries.

Regarding the former, there are now more ways for MBAs to use their skills in this environment than there were a decade or so ago. MBAs can bring expertise in organizational planning, development, and management. Charter schools often welcome individuals with business skills who can help with the operations and finance activities required to succeed. In addition, some reform-oriented public school superintendents might take on an MBA to help in these areas. The easiest entry into this field currently tends to be through school management companies, which are often run by MBAs or former businesspeople more prone to hire those with similar skill sets.

However, finding opportunities in K-12 education will require more investigation than the typical job search. MBAs who want to work in public education should be aware that many educators are concerned that MBAs fall short on instructional skills and experience, understanding, and leadership—and therefore are less likely to recognize the MBA's value in their organization. Nonetheless, some MBAs have successfully started their own charter schools (see profile of Stacey Boyd, in chapter 2) and others have worked within existing schools (see profile of Monique Burns in this chapter). Furthermore, the field of higher education has abundant positions in fundraising, admissions, and administration (see profile of Bob Fogel in this chapter).

In the larger marketplace of education-related services, interested MBAs should select their area of focus, be it curricula, technology, etc., and contact the major organizations in the field. Entry-level positions there, comparable to those in some other industries, involve marketing, strategic planning, operations, or finance.

For additional resources and addresses of education organizations, see the Resource Road Map.

MONIQUE BURNS

Becoming a public school administrator

Monique Burns (Harvard Business School, MBA 1993) knew early on in her career that she wanted to use her skills to improve the nation's education system. "My first job out of college was in marketing and brand management at Quaker Oats. I loved the intellectual stimulation of working with smart people on fun and interesting business problems, but I realized that 'selling junk food to dogs' (as assistant brand manager of Snausages and Pupperoni dog treats) was not my life's calling." Burns was inspired by the tutoring program in which Quaker Oats encouraged its employees to be involved. "Two days a week, I volunteered with local inner-city school children. I saw how bright, capable, street-smart, and savvy they were, and was frustrated by the lack of support these kids received from adults."

Burns also volunteered in an urban magnet school that partnered with her undergraduate alumni association. One day, the principal mentioned that the children were not using the fourth floor of the building because there was a hole in the roof. "I immediately assumed this was because the school didn't have the funds to repair it. To my dismay, the principal responded that money was not the issue; rather, it was simply that the school district had only authorized so many roofing contractors to fix such problems and that there was a three-and-a-half-year waiting list at the central office. This never would have happened at Quaker Oats! I said to myself, 'something here is wrong.'"

Burns came to business school because she wanted to build the skills required to create a supportive school infrastructure. When the time came to find a summer job, she realized she had no foothold in the education industry. "I met with several faculty members to get names and contacts in the field. Through them, I made contact with the Council for Chief State School Officers in Washington, D.C.—the lobbying arm of the country's state school superintendents—where I decided to work for the summer." While there, Burns met with and interviewed people at every national education group, think tank, and consulting firm in the greater Washington, D.C., area.

During her second year of the MBA program, Burns focused on courses in organizational change. She remembers courses such as Power and Influence, Designing, Managing, and Improving Organizations, Service Management, and Change Management as critical to her understanding of how she would be able to help manage schools. She also cross-registered at the Harvard Graduate School of Education to learn more about education reform. An independent research project helping the public schools in Washington, D.C. with program evaluation helped her develop expertise and further her network in the field.

"My first job after graduation was with an education consulting group in Washington, D.C. It had contracted with the public school system to open four state-of-the-art middle schools in the District. Though I did not have much educational experience, I did have operational experience, and this was how I marketed myself. They partnered me with a veteran educator and we got things done. After a year with the consulting group, I signed on to work with the superintendent directly. Basically, I wanted to work in a school and get an understanding of what is going on 'in the trenches,' and the superinten-

dent wanted a site-based budgeting pilot run in nine schools. So I ran his budgeting pilot and he appointed me to be an assistant to the principal in one of the three middle schools I had opened.

Burns worked with a gifted principal at the school and loved the experience. However, she was looking for an opportunity to have an impact on a larger scale and in a school system where she could truly make a difference. Her business school network came into the picture again at that point. "I was doing an admissions presentation for HBS in Washington (as a former admissions office staffer, she was asked to do this on occasion). And I met a prospective student there who connected me with my next job—working for the new superintendent of schools in Philadelphia."

Burns became a special assistant to the superintendent for management and productivity. "My job was to monitor the implementation of recommendations made by the private business sector in Philadelphia to aid the school district in improving services and saving $50 million annually on the delivery of its support services (facilities, human resources, food service, transportation, and purchasing). My MBA skills in negotiations and operations management helped me to think through the district's problems and work with the different departments to help them consider new processes. I established myself as a truth-telling, no-nonsense arbitrator who could work well with everyone from the business community to the unionized janitors." Despite this success, Burns still felt that she wasn't fully accepted by a powerful group of stakeholders—the teachers. "If you haven't taught or you don't have your master's degree in education, they become very leery of you."

"I established myself as a truth-telling, no-nonsense arbitrator who could work well with everyone from the business community to the unionized janitors."

With that in mind, Burns knew what she needed to do next. She returned to Harvard to pursue a doctoral degree at the Graduate School of Education. Her next step? Burns dreams of running her own school district. With the combination of business and education credentials, she is extremely well-positioned to succeed.

BOB FOGEL

Educating executives

"It's total luck that I ended up here, but I'm having a great time," says Bob Fogel (Harvard Business School, MBA 1991), executive director of the Harvard Business School's Executive Education program. "This job is just like being CEO of my own business—I get to manage hands-on, handle finances, and oversee organizational growth and change, marketing, corporate relations, etc. Plus, it has a mission I can identify with."

Fogel's long and circuitous path to his current position began at the Coast Guard Academy, followed by twelve years as an officer in the Coast Guard. While he chose the academy primarily because of the scholarship it offered him, he stayed with the Coast Guard because he liked the idea of saving lives and improving drug law enforcement. Drug policy had a special significance for him, since his brother's drug addiction "almost tore the family apart."

As a Coast Guard officer, Fogel had a broad range of jobs and experiences. One of his first assignments was as a captain of a Coast Guard ship off the coast of Florida, undertaking drug raids and basically "being paid to be John Wayne." At twenty-three, he was appointed captain of a ship out of Miami, Florida, one that "was a total basketcase." Although in charge of the entire crew, he was significantly younger than many of his men, including two of his direct reports. "I thought that I should show them who was in charge, and then I realized that they let me be in charge." Overall, Fogel reflects, he "made a lot of mistakes as captain of that ship and was taken to task for it." But Fogel credits the experience with exposing him to leadership at an unusually early age. And he learned quickly: within two years, his boat was the most successful boat in the Coast Guard.

After those two years, Fogel served as an admirals' assistant in Miami, working with George Bush's Vice Presidential Task Force on drug law enforcement. There, he saw "a much bigger picture" of drug policy, including the tradeoffs between enforcement (operating on the supply side) and education (affecting the demand side). He also gained insight into the political machinations of Washington, D.C., and found a role model. One of the admirals to whom he reported was "an amazing leader. He could relate to everyone from the heads of state to the regular guys on the ship. He even changed his language and mannerisms with different people."

At that time the Coast Guard was facing budget constraints, and there was talk about sending some people to business school to learn finance. Fogel applied to and was accepted to HBS. (He found out later that he was a "test case" for the Admissions Committee, which didn't know how to evaluate a Coast Guard application.)

At HBS, Fogel was elected education representative for his section and remained very involved with educational initiatives both years. He found a friend in Professor Earl Sasser, then chair of the MBA program, who was to play an important role in Fogel's later career. "When the Berlin Wall came down, Earl was really excited about exploring what happens when countries need to change from Communism to capitalism overnight. He had the idea that MBA students should take two days out of their regular course schedules to reflect on that transition. We organized this huge event, with political leaders from Eastern Europe, experts from Harvard, and students all discussing the implications of the collapse of Communism."

When Fogel returned to the Coast Guard after business school, he found that he didn't like the CFO job. "In contrast to what I'd done before, and in business school, it was too narrow. . . . I knew I needed to stay there ten years to move up, but also knew that I didn't want to be an admiral anyway. So I started thinking about other things to do." He considered consulting and sought the guidance of Sasser, who advised him against any firm that would be reluctant to bring him in at a managerial level. On that recommendation, he joined Coopers & Lybrand as a senior manager. Although he found the

> *"I need to like what I do, and I need to feel like I'm making a difference. Luckily I have both where I am right now."*

work interesting and fun, Fogel knew within a year that consulting wasn't for him.

Proving that both connections and luck play instrumental roles in one's career, Earl Sasser called him "out of the blue" six months later, saying that he had a spot open in Executive Education. Fogel hesitated because of the pay cut and his lack of focus, up to that point, on the field of education. On the other hand, he knew a lot of people at HBS who were eager for him to come. He decided to try it.

As of 1998, Fogel has helped grow Executive Education from 1,800 to 7,000 participants. He feels that a successful Executive Education program enhances, rather than detracts from, the school's mission. As he explains it, the mission of HBS is twofold: to groom leaders and help them grow to their full potential, and to make an impact on the practice of management. Since professors are responsible for a large part of this mission, both through teaching and writing, they must remain in touch with business practitioners. If not, he worries, faculty will lose touch with what is current and important in management. At the same time, Fogel recognizes the need to keep a balance between the school's programs

and stresses that Executive Education is nearing the end of its growth spurt. Instead, he is now investigating new areas—such as customized programs with specific companies—that can benefit both teaching and learning at HBS.

While he has invested considerable time in leading the program's growth, Fogel emphasizes that a large and satisfying part of his job is "being a coach." When he arrived at Executive Education, he notes, "it was almost like a family business. There was tremendous loyalty to the organization. Yet at the same time, many employees did not have up-to-date skills in terms of technology." Since Fogel knew that dedication was a rare quality, he made the decision to invest in training for his employees to build upon the family business environment while simultaneously improving professionalism, thereby creating a mosaic whose sum is greater than the individual parts.

Fogel's diverse experiences have led him to a job he enjoys and a simple explanation for career satisfaction. "I need to like what I do, and I need to feel like I'm making a difference. Luckily I have both where I am right now."

Environment

Overview

Environmental social enterprise organizations defy easy categorization. Some work internationally, others nationally, regionally, locally, or on multiple levels. One way to think about the kind of organization in which you would want to work is to consider the primary strategy that the nonprofit uses and the issues it addresses. Recognize, however, that many employ a mix of techniques—including research, outreach, education, negotiations, and lobbying—to achieve their goals.

Subdivisions

Advocacy Groups
Advocacy groups are a prominent category within the environment subsector. Greenpeace and Sierra Club are probably the best-known examples, but thousands of other organizations inform and rally the public and politi-

cians around issues and policies. Some tackle a single concern, some multiple issues. Alliance building is popular: for example, the Southern Utah Wilderness Alliance and the Greater Yellowstone Coalition serve as umbrella groups for several other nonprofits that share their goals. Advocacy groups range in staff size from a few people to hundreds. These organizations also tend to have a strong membership base.

Policy Research Organizations
Policy organizations are a second broad category. Groups like Resources for the Future and the World Resources Institute produce bipartisan analysis and provide recommendations to policy makers at top levels of government. Staffs often include scientists, lawyers, economists, and public policy graduates. Foundations, corporations, and major donors provide a significant percentage of the financial support.

A subset of policy research organizations, such as the Environmental Defense Fund, Natural Resources Defense Council, and the Conservation Law Foundation, uses the courts as a means to stop pollution and create stronger environmental policy. Others, like Keystone Center, are distinguished by their emphasis on negotiation and consensus building.

Preservation and Land Trusts

This category includes organizations that use conservation easements, land donations and purchases, and estate planning to protect open space. Financial and real estate expertise and an ability to organize communities and landowners to preserve areas threatened by sprawl and development are special staff skills. Organizations in this category include the Trust for Public Land and The Nature Conservancy.

Educational Institutions

Educational institutions include schools, museums, zoos, parks, botanical gardens, and field schools. Such organizations educate the public on environmental issues and behaviors and hire environmental teachers, curriculum writers, and financial managers to maximize their effectiveness.

Environmental Responsibility and "Green Marketing"

Increasingly, companies employ these two terms to demonstrate their commitment to the environment. While jobs of this sort fall into the category of socially responsible businesses rather than environmental social enterprises, they do offer opportunities for MBAs with an interest in the environment.

Hot Topics

Corporate Environmentalism. Nonprofits are developing partnerships with companies to help them reduce waste, prevent pollution, conserve resources, and enhance business performance. The Coalition for Environmentally Responsible Economies, the Environmental Defense Fund, and the Management Institute for Environment and Business are all organizations that design responsible policies and encourage businesses to view environmental solutions in strategic, not just compliance, terms.

Decentralized, Consensus-Based Action. The focus of the environmental movement has shifted to the state and local levels. Nonprofits want to build community support for environmental solutions to produce a broad-based constituency that pursues its own goals, not a constituency that supports someone else's agenda. Priorities include negotiating local plans for land management and enlisting the support of diverse stakeholders—resource users, businesses, and environmentalists—in management plans.

Environmental Ethics. Almost every nonprofit environmental group is worried about the ethical dimensions of environmental issues. They wrestle with the challenge of balancing the needs of current generations with those of future citizens, particularly with regard to the uncertain and highly risky impacts of climate change and nuclear waste. Equity concerns are a related "hot topic." For example, the impacts of higher gasoline taxes, proposed as a way to reduce air pollution, could fall more heavily on the poor. Similarly, poor and racial minorities tend to be the groups most exposed to pollution in the United States.

Mobilizing a Diverse Constituency. Many organizations are seeking ways to help minorities gain a stronger voice in environmental decisions. City dwellers are another undermobilized constituency, even though they represent the majority of the population and face some of the most serious environmental problems worldwide. Many in the field are concerned that people in their twenties and thirties are taking less of an activist role than in prior decades.

Market-Based Incentives. Though this issue has been around since the 1980s, it remains a major part of environmental policy. After centralized regulation limited large "point sources" of pollution in the 1970s and 1980s, nonprofits, the government, and the public became interested in finding more creative, cost-effective ways to reduce pollution—such as applying market-based incentives to environmental concerns. Finding ways to implement tradable permit systems, green taxes, environmental accounting systems, and other market-based pollution control regimes nationally and internationally continues to be a priority for many organizations.

Roles for MBAs

A new era in environmentalism has created a wealth of opportunities for business school graduates to contribute meaningfully to this part of the nonprofit sector. Environmental groups are succeeding by promoting solutions and policies that incorporate economic and sustainable development goals. The ability to work with—rather than against—the private sector has become essential. And, as the number of environmental groups has skyrocketed, many of them are recognizing that they need to change how they operate internally. Better financial and strategic management is proving critical to stretching limited dollars, distinguishing their work, and achieving maximum impact.

Correspondingly, employers need people with a clear grasp of micro- and macroeconomics, statistics, and finance. Business savvy, an understanding of the science underlying environmental issues, and public policy and management skills make a very strong job candidate. In addition, like many nonprofit organizations, almost every nonprofit environmental group needs development staff and talented public relations people, which creates many opportunities for good writers. Having business acumen helps—once you know the language of the issues, you need to make a clear and compelling case to key audiences, often in the corporate world. Also, as mentioned previously, many corporations will hire MBAs with special knowledge of environmental issues and green products for environmental marketing positions.

For additional resources and addresses of environmental organizations, see the Resource Road Map.

ANDREW KENDALL

Building a natural sanctuary

"How would you like to work on the most ambitious project in our organization's 100-year history?" The president's words lingered in Andy Kendall's ears. Just prior to meeting with the president of the Massachusetts Audubon Society (MAS), Kendall (Harvard Business School, MBA 1988) had been ready to accept a job heading up the Latin American operations of a local power company. The offer before him, however, was too good to pass up.

Kendall accepted the offer to become the MAS director of Boston programs and to spearhead the creation of the Boston Nature Center and Wildlife Sanctuary, the first inner-city nature center of its kind. Turning the dream of the Boston Nature Center and Wildlife Sanctuary into a reality has involved everything from raising several million dollars from foundations, individuals, and organizations to negotiating site plans with local officials.

"There are so many job opportunities, so many ways to go. You're only limited by your imagination."

The center will be situated on seventy acres in the heart of Boston at the former Boston State Hospital site. It will include space for meetings, workshops, wildlife exhibits, and nature classes. In addition, MAS will provide outdoor environmental education and training programs for youth, adults, and families at the site. The center will place a strong emphasis on reaching the more than 24,000 Boston schoolchildren located within a two-mile radius. Once it is operational, the center will be a national model for environmental groups across the nation.

Kendall is grateful for the opportunity he has had to create and shape this exciting center. Since he grew up in the Boston area, the work has given him a chance to give back to his community while also gaining experience working with state and city officials, local organizations, and community groups. "It's been an exciting, high visibility project," Kendall states as he points to a *Boston Globe* article featuring his picture and a description of the center.

Kendall is able to draw on his MBA and prior work experiences to address the daily challenges of the job. Prior to business school, Kendall worked at an animal feed manufacturing company in Arizona. His interest in small- and medium-sized manufacturing companies continued throughout his years at business school. Since on-campus recruiting focused primarily on larger companies in the financial and consulting industries, Kendall "shunned the traditional MBA job search." Instead, he conducted his own search, using the alumni network to set up informational interviews throughout New England.

While conducting his search, Kendall decided to interview with Lincoln Electric. "It was the only one that interested me, and I was particularly impressed with Don Hastings, the president of the company." Kendall was one of four HBS graduates hired by the company to "shake up the organization." He shaped his own training program in an effort to gain exposure to all facets of the company—from building welding equipment on the assembly line to selling in the field. After his training, Kendall designed and implemented a nationwide network of distribution centers.

"By then it was 1990. I had been with the company a little over two years, and I was starting to question whether this is what I wanted to continue doing." The long hours prevented him from developing other parts of life, namely his interest in the environment and giving back to the community. "I was working myself to death in a pressure cooker. I could continue to do so and work up the ladder, but what would I have really done?" He loved the environment and the outdoors and had some experience working with nonprofits while at business school and at Lincoln Electric. And he began to question how he could bring together his interest in the environment and his business skills.

"I decided to quit my job, and I spent three months interviewing the CEOs of environmental organizations from the grass-roots to the big nationals." Based on these interviews, he decided that the real action was at the state level—the national organizations felt too removed for his tastes. "At the state level, you have an opportunity to be a big fish in a small pond." Not long after his interviews, Kendall accepted a job as CFO of the New Hampshire Audubon Society. He helped the organization address a financial crisis and gain stability. He later became the organization's executive vice president.

"Business, management, and finance were my entrée—allowing me to get my foot in the door. In exchange, I asked the organization to allow me to get involved in substantive, program issues. . . . You've got to be involved in the program side. You don't want to be branded as just the finance person or the MBA."

After about three years with the New Hampshire Audubon Society, Kendall and his wife decided to take time to travel and work abroad. He spent a considerable amount of time in Latin America, where he provided consulting assistance to a number of organizations interested in environmentally sustainable energy. During this time, he also consulted to the Massachusetts Audubon Society on a project in Costa Rica. "This was my equivalent to a scientist's field work. I had to shake the bonds of finance and administration and develop my own substantive project work." Such project work would give him the credibility he sought to develop on the program side of nonprofit work.

Shortly after he returned from his work abroad, MAS offered him the director of Boston Programs position. "The Boston Nature Center and Wildlife Sanctuary has served as a springboard to help me learn more about MAS. . . . It really is a great organization with a lot of opportunity."

His advice to students embarking on independent job searches: "Be patient and persevere. . . . It will pay off. There are so many job opportunities, so many ways to go. You're only limited by your imagination. You only need to look at the alumni books to see all the opportunities that are out there. It's actually the minority of alumni who are in the so-called traditional MBA careers."

Foundations

Overview

The Foundation Center defines a foundation as a nonprofit, nongovernmental organization with an endowment of its own that serves the public good (and therefore qualifies for tax-exempt status) primarily by providing grants to other nonprofit organizations. Foundations have two primary sets of activities: endowment management (portfolio managers invest foundation assets to increase the endowment) and grant-making (program managers review grant applications and determine who will receive grants). To maintain their tax-exempt status most founda-tions are required to give away at least 5 percent of their endowment each year to nonprofit organizations (called a "payout requirement").

There are more than 40,000 foundations in the United States alone, though one-third of that total controls 90 percent of all foundation assets. In 1997, foundations gave away nearly $12.3 billion in grants to other nonprofit organizations and individuals and managed over $230 billion in assets. Foundations vary widely in size, but most of them fall into the category of "assets under $1 million."

Many foundations choose to focus their grant-giving on specific program areas. For example, the Packard Foundation has a strong focus on children, the Soros Foundation specializes in international issues, and the Robert Wood Johnson Foundation emphasizes health. Other foundations are even more specialized. For example, the Massachusetts Environmental Trust gives grants to environmental nonprofits that take "innovative approaches to protecting and preserving the Commonwealth's natural resources."

Subdivisions

Private/Independent Foundations
These are usually founded by one individual, often by bequest. Many large independent foundations are run by boards and staff outside the original donor's family. Most of the very large foundations are private/independent. Private foundations include the Ford Foundation, the Rockefeller Foundation, and the John D. and Catherine T. MacArthur Foundation.

Family Foundations
Though not a legal term, a family foundation is one that is either managed or strongly influenced by the original donor or members of the donor's family. Most are small, with less than $5 million in assets.

Community Foundations
These foundations are usually focused on specific geographic areas and build their endowments through contributions from a variety of sources within the community. The Internal Revenue Service designates community foundations as public charities rather than private foundations because they raise a significant portion of their resources from a broad cross-section of the public each year. There are approximately 300 community foundations today, including the Boston Foundation, the Cleveland Foundation, and the New York Community Trust.

Corporate Foundations
Companies can (and do) establish foundations, funded by a combination of an initial endowment and periodic contributions from corporate profits. The foundations are tax exempt as long as they are legally separate from the parent company (as compared to corporate giving programs, which are not separate entities). Corporate community relations officers (see profile of Nancy Lane later in this chapter) are a close but distinctly different relative of corporate foundation officers.

Operating Foundations
Operating foundations (such as the Getty Trust and the Carnegie Endowment for International Peace) are private foundations that use the majority of their endowment income to provide services rather than to make grants.

Hot Topics

Measuring the Impact of Grants. Since the primary function of a foundation is to give grants to other organizations, evaluating the worthiness and potential social return of grant recipients is a key role. Measuring impact (otherwise known as outcomes analysis) can have several dimensions: the effectiveness of the grantee in using the foundation's funds, the impact of the program on the targeted issue, and the effectiveness of the foundation's work overall. Outcomes analysis is a difficult field, especially when social outcomes are the primary measures of success.

Encouraging Collaboration. Increasingly, foundations have encouraged collaboration among grantees, in part to avoid overlap of services in the community. However, there is a delicate balance between encouraging grantees to collaborate and becoming overly directive. Collaboration is sometimes difficult because nonprofits do compete with one another for funds from several sources.

Program-Related Investments (PRIs). A PRI is a loan, loan guarantee, or other investment (rather than an outright donation of money) made by a foundation for a specific project. PRIs are often made from a revolving fund, and the foundation expects to receive its money back, usually without interest or at below-market rates. PRIs allow foundations to "recycle" funds to assist a greater number of nonprofit organizations, and they encourage charities to become somewhat less reliant on grants and to operate in a more financially responsible manner.

Foundations as Venture Capitalists. Comparisons have been made between the role of foundations in the nonprofit world and the role of venture-capital firms in the for-profit world, since both help organizations bring program/product ideas to market. Unlike venture-capital firms, foundations traditionally play a hands-off role—giving short-term grants for programs as requested in grant applications. However, there is increasing pressure for foundations to consider longer-term grants, grants and/or consulting assistance to help nonprofits develop greater management capacity, and in general to play a greater role in risk management through hands-on involvement with grantees (similar to venture-capital firms' board seats on portfolio companies).

Roles for MBAs

The foundations field is difficult to break into professionally. Connections are critical. That said, there are many potential roles for MBAs, whose analytical skills are highly valued in foundation work. Managing the foundation's endowment is a role naturally attractive to many MBAs, since they can directly apply their business skills to the work (see profile of Kim Lew later in this chapter).

Program management jobs are harder to come by, since they often require fairly deep knowledge of an issue area. However, with some experience in a program area, or after breaking into the foundation ranks in another role, MBAs can move into this area as well.

For additional resources and addresses of foundations, see the Resource Road Map.

KIM LEW

Investing well to give more

Kim Lew (Harvard Business School, MBA 1992) spends her days as a portfolio strategist for the Ford Foundation analyzing companies in the technology sector, making investment decisions for a portion of the foundation's $10-billion endowment (over $4 billion of which is in internally managed equities). "My decisions make the foundation's assets grow so that they can give grants to organizations that are making the community a better place to live." Lew had spent a year and a half after business school in private placement at Prudential Insurance Company of America, but found that it was only after she left work each day that she was able to pursue her true interests and find fulfillment through volunteering and other community activities. In contrast, she says, "I love my job at the Ford Foundation. I totally support the basic mission of the organization. I like both the work I do and the reason for doing it."

The investment side of the foundation "business" supports the primary focus: the program side. The better the investments, the more there is to give in grants. "I make the same types of buy/sell decisions as an investment analyst at Fidelity Investments does, but I'm doing it for the foundation, which to me means a lot more." But at a foundation, this role brings some different challenges than it does in the finance world at large, such as the need to consider a company's record on diversity and other social responsibility considerations. But ultimately, investment decisions are based on sound company fundamentals.

Lew notes that it is significantly easier for MBAs to get jobs on the investment side of a foundation, since the link between the MBA education and the demands of the job are so clear. "My business school background made a big difference when I began to think about analyzing industries and companies for the endowment. The case study method in particular taught me to make good decisions with limited information—which is what a portfolio manager always has to do."

> *"The case study method in particular taught me to make good decisions with limited information—which is what a portfolio manager always has to do."*

Lew feels that her MBA degree is valued more at the Ford Foundation because it is less common than it would be in a corporation. Though she came to the foundation with a very strong skill set developed as an undergraduate at the Wharton School and through her prebusiness school experience in middle-market lending at Chemical Bank, her MBA provided a certain level of immediate credibility when Lew arrived as a fairly young new hire in the division.

Getting a job on the program side of a foundation presents more of a challenge to MBAs, unless they have significant experience in a program area. Three broad program areas guide Ford's grant-making decisions: (1) education, media, arts, and culture (including diversity efforts); (2) asset building and community development (including poverty eradication, economic development, reproductive health, and program-related investments; and (3) peace and social justice/civil rights (including worldwide efforts to promote human rights).

With an endowment of over $10 billion, the Ford Foundation gives away at least $550 million per year to meet the payout requirement. "So you see why our grants tend to be quite large, since giving away a few thousand at a time would be costly and inefficient. We tend to work with larger organizations and only fund national (not local/community) initiatives, with a few exceptions."

"Program officers at Ford have extensive experience and expertise in their program areas. Most have run organizations in the field, or have done significant research, or both, and can say, 'I know that X, Y, or Z needs to be done.' They also have fairly extensive networks of contacts in the field." Some MBAs have been able to make their way into the program side over time. At Ford, Lew notes, the PRI group (program-related investments are loans rather than grants) is made up of mostly MBAs, because they know how to evaluate and make loans to organizations. Other MBAs win a position at Ford because of prior program-related experience. "Program experience is more critical at Ford and other large foundations because of the size of the grants and the proactive role we play. Ford takes a very active role with grantees because we give at such a high level. In essence, program officers research and develop ideas and then find organizations to carry them out. Thus they need experience and contacts in their program area to do their job well." This is a big difference between the large and the small foundations.

However, Lew has had the opportunity to dip her toe into grant-making as a member of Ford's "Good Neighbor Committee," a group that reviews neighborhood-based grant applications (the New York City neighborhood is the area from 34th Street to 50th Street, river to river). The committee includes staff from all of the support functions of the foundation (such as investments, administration, legal, etc.) and is chaired by someone

from the program side "to keep an eye on us." Lew's involvement "has been a great way for me to learn the program side and to see some terrific community projects get off the ground." The Good Neighbor Program is one of the few grant programs that gives fairly small grants to community organizations, but it is also very important for the foundation because it keeps staff in touch with what is going on in their backyard.

Lew's MBA skill set has helped in her day-to-day work, but her business school network helped her get the foundation job in the first place. "I had made the conscious decision to leave my job at Prudential because I just wasn't happy there. I knew I wanted to be in New York, and I wanted to gain more experience working with organizations engaged in economic development. It just happened that the mother of my "HBS little brother" (Perry Fagan, Harvard Business School, MBA 1993 and Lew's mentee) was the director of equity research at the Ford Foundation and was looking to hire someone. Even though I didn't have equity experience, my connection to Perry and my MBA convinced her to interview me. We hit it off, and I got the job—and learned a lot about equities very quickly."

Lew's social enterprise commitment extends well beyond the workplace. She serves as treasurer and chief financial officer on the working board of an arts gallery in Newark, New Jersey, and is an active board member of PACE (Program for the Acceleration of Careers in Engineering), a nonprofit organization that helps high school students of color in Brooklyn learn science, math, and general leadership skills. She also teaches PACE leadership classes on Saturday mornings and volunteers as a mentor for Business Leadership for Tomorrow (a nonprofit started by John Rice, Harvard Business School, MBA 1992, that matches college students with MBA mentors—see profile later in this chapter).

Government/Public Sector

Overview

We could have dedicated an entire guide to careers in the public sector. Instead, this section will provide a high-level overview of public sector opportunities and describe

the challenges of finding jobs and working in government.

Within the government you can work on the federal, state, or local level. At each level, in addition to elected positions (including U.S. President, senator, state representative), government jobs can be divided into three general categories: (1) career service (competitive service);

(2) political appointment; and (3) exempted service. Despite this simple description, the reality is that government systems are extremely complex. Given this complexity, locating meaningful employment in a federal, state, or local agency or legislature can be a challenging, confusing, frustrating exercise. It can also be an exciting experience and an opportunity to develop interesting and valuable contacts in a world where relationships are the cornerstones for decisions and deals at every level. To build this network of contacts, job seekers must have at least some background knowledge of the structure of government and of the types of opportunities available for an MBA looking to make a difference.

Subdivisions

Federal Government
Consider this company prospectus: the U.S. government operates on an annual budget of $1.5 trillion, channeling those funds to more than 83,000 state and local governments, 150 countries, and the vendors, contractors, and community-based organizations that make up the private sector. To accomplish this, Uncle Sam employs almost 3 million civilians working in over 100 federal agencies in the three branches of government—not to mention the two million military personnel charged with protecting our national security. The management, finance, and marketing opportunities are vast. Within the government are three main job categories:

- *Career positions* are those based on merit rather than political connections. Such positions include policy advisors and budget analysts working in all federal agencies, including positions in cabinet-level agencies (the Department of the Interior, Department of the Treasury, etc.), and independent agencies (a level below the cabinet, such as the Environmental Protection Agency [EPA]). The majority of jobs in the federal government fall into this category.

- *Appointed positions* (appointed by the President) account for approximately 2,000 of the almost three million civil service positions. Those jobs tend to be reserved for loyal campaign footsoldiers, skilled professionals with excellent political contacts, and whomever else the President and his advisors deem worthy and appropriate. Appointed positions include the cabinet secretaries and other top-level professionals requiring Senate confirmation. Such positions often involve an interesting blend of policy analysis and political judgment. Of course, the biggest downside to a political appointment is that when the administration in power is voted out, so are you.

- *Exempted service* refers to those agencies that fall outside the authority of the Office of Personnel Management (OPM), the agency that oversees the federal government's personnel functions. These exempted agencies include Congress, federal courts, the Central Intelligence Agency (CIA), the National Security Agency, the Federal Bureau of Investigation (FBI), the Department of State, and the Secret Service. Jobs in these agencies are not subject to the formal OPM hiring standards or procedures, or the General Schedule (GS) pay scale, which sets the salaries for all career service positions. Interestingly, the skills needed to obtain exempted service and career positions are the same as those needed to land a political appointment: research, networking, and relationship building.

Jobs on Capitol Hill (the House of Representatives and the Senate) fall into the exempted category and may be of interest to MBAs. You can work on a congressional committee or in a member's personal office. If you are not willing or able to work in Washington, keep in mind that each representative and senator has an office in his or her home district. Those jobs tend to be less policy-oriented and more constituent service-oriented.

If you have a particular expertise in a policy area, research relevant congressional committees. Committees are much more insulated from the day-to-day constituent service done in the personal offices of individual members. Consequently, these staffs craft legislation and public policy considered by the committees, which is then taken to the House or Senate floor for a vote. Almost every piece of legislation must go through a committee, including the all-important budget and appropriations bills. However, most committee staffs are made up of seasoned professionals with advanced degrees and Capitol Hill experience.

State and Local Government
Positions on the state and local level are similar to those on the federal level. In most states, the governor is the parallel office to the U.S. President, and state agencies (such as the Massachusetts Department of Public Health) mirror agencies on the federal level as well. In many regions, state and local governments remain fragmented structures, with dizzying arrays of agencies, departments, commissions, and councils. Like Congress, state legislatures provide job opportunities on members' staffs and on committees.

In addition to the personal offices of individual members and committee staffs, larger states tend to have support offices that offer legislative analysis, bill drafting, research, and budget and audit services. While there is still no well-developed hiring system, these offices mean greater employment opportunities for those who want to work closely with legislation at the state level. As on Capitol Hill, job hunting means contacting legislators directly, getting to know their staffs, and volunteering on a campaign when feasible.

Hot Topics

Devolution. With the federal government increasingly shifting responsibilities downward in a "devolution revolution," important policy-making roles and management jobs are shifting to state capitals and city halls. In the past several years, shrinking federal resources have spawned new and creative approaches to funding important government programs. Increasingly, states and cities are viewed by top-level policy makers as the nation's laboratories for innovative and cost-saving solutions, and block grants are one of the new tools giving local policy makers freedom to experiment.

Consequently, the "devolution revolution" is shining the spotlight on state and local government, forcing agencies at every level to professionalize their hiring practices and attract skilled, well-educated policy analysts and managers. According to Ronald and Caryl Krannich in their *Complete Guide to Public Employment* (see Resource Road Map), "governors have more power, bureaucrats are more professional, and civil services regulate the hiring and firing of personnel."

Adoption of Private Sector Practices. The style of government is shifting, as exemplified by the fact that "reinvention," "customer service," and "private sector practices" are terms now fully integrated into the bureaucratic lexicon. In fact, Vice President Al Gore's report to the nation on his reinvention efforts was entitled, "Businesslike Government: Lessons Learned from America's Best Companies." This shift in style also means something very important for business school graduates interested in government service. Effective managers, innovative thinkers, and creative policy makers are in demand! On the state and local level, legislatures have become significantly more professionalized, many moving from part-time to full-time, operating most of the year and with staff resources similar to those on Capitol Hill. This trend on all levels makes MBA skills more highly valued in the government.

Roles for MBAs

While the Office of Personnel Management oversees a formal hiring process for all federal career positions, which includes posting vacancy announcements on the Internet (<www.usajobs.opm.gov>) and in federal offices, individual agencies are responsible for hiring their own staffs. Since the 1980s, the federal hiring system has become increasingly decentralized, which is actually to the job seeker's advantage. Thus, the first step in any federal job search must be to identify agencies of interest and then request an informational interview with the person in charge of hiring—the key decision maker in the specific agency, division, or bureau—so that when job openings occur, you are first on their list of people to call. The names of key people can easily be found in numerous federal directories in the library or in your school's career services office. *The Federal Yellow Book* and *Carroll's Federal Directory* are just two volumes chock-full of information. These companies also publish similar directories for Congress, states, federal regional offices, and municipalities. On Capitol Hill, each congressional office does its own interviewing and hiring. Narrowing your target list down to those politicians representing your geographic and policy interest areas will give the greatest likelihood of success in the job search.

On the state and local levels, job seekers must be prepared to research and network extensively, using similar strategies to the federal job search. Identify the people in charge of hiring in your chosen agencies, most likely the chiefs of staff, and ask for informational interviews. As in the federal government, only go through the personnel office for the formal aspects of the job search, such as responding to official postings and filling out appropriate forms. Remember: your goal is to find out about openings before they are posted. It is also important to keep in mind that while political connections still play a strong role in hiring at the state and local levels, it is not always appropriate to use your political clout. Your research should give you a good sense of the key people and overall culture of the agencies.

Several special federal and state employment programs, such as the Presidential Management Internship Program, the White House Fellows Program, and the Senior Executive Service offer a "fast track" to government employment for talented individuals coming out of graduate school (often schools of government or policy, but MBAs are eligible as well).

For additional resources and addresses of government organizations and fellowship programs, see the Resource Road Map.

FREDERICK W. ALLEN

An MBA in the federal government

In government, as in private business, "you are dealing with an entity that has resources that must be managed to accomplish a goal," explains Frederick W. (Derry) Allen (Harvard Business School, MBA 1973), who has been in federal service for twenty-five years. Currently the counselor to the assistant administrator for policy at the EPA, Allen has held a number of positions in this and other federal agencies. His first job out of business school was at the Cost of Living Council, which regulated wages and prices under President Nixon in the 1970s.

Throughout these experiences, Allen used the management, planning, budgeting, and accounting skills he learned at business school. "Nothing in government is as simple as 'turning a profit,'" he explains, noting that private business is just beginning to understand the plight of the public sector. "You have to serve many, many masters here."

Allen characterizes MBAs who choose public sector employment as "mission-driven," and that was certainly true for him. Prior to business school, Allen worked for two years as a VISTA volunteer in the New York City Department of Corrections. While at business school, he found a number of professors interested in public policy. After graduation he joined two of his HBS classmates at the Cost of Living Council (CLC), whose director at the time was Harvard Economist John Dunlop.

Dunlop later became U.S. secretary of labor, and Allen and some of his colleagues joined the secretary's staff.

After twenty years at the EPA, Allen reminisces, "I stayed here because of the opportunity to do interesting, important work, and because the EPA has a highly skilled group of people. It doesn't conform to the stereotypes of a dead government bureaucracy," he explains. He relishes his role in planning the nation's environmental policy, measuring its progress, and looking ahead to future environmental issues. He sees his work "[touching] so many aspects of not only life in this country, but other countries as well." He has also seen a sea change in the way government does business, with a greater emphasis on customer service and a market-oriented approach, business school concepts that were at one time foreign to the public sector. "We're not turning a profit, but if you interpret the word 'profit' in a broader sense, we are."

"You have to serve many, many masters here."

Allen sees no particular magic in landing a good policy or management job in the federal government, though he does recognize the critical nature of the networked job search. He recites a familiar refrain: "Pound the pavement . . . and use your network." But most of all, as with many social sector careers, "You have to want it . . . the opportunity to make a difference is there—that's what has to keep you going."

Health Care

Overview

Health care is by far the largest segment of the nonprofit service sector. According to the Foundation Center, in 1989 nonprofit health providers accounted for over 60 percent of all nonprofit revenues. In the context of the medical model, health care comprises disease and disability prevention (such as immunization for measles), treatment (such as an appendectomy for appendicitis), and palliation (as with pain control in terminal cancer). In re-cent years there has been increasing emphasis placed on health promotion (which involves empowering people to improve their own health) and on the broad determinants of health.

From a career perspective, the health-care field can also be segmented by type of organization: direct care providers, services supporting provision of care, insurers, public health organizations, and medical supply and device manufacturers. Organizations and service providers can be for-profit, nonprofit, public, private, or some combination of the above. Many social service agencies are involved in prevention and health-care services as well.

Subdivisions

Direct Care Providers

There is a wide range of direct care providers, including acute-care hospitals, rehabilitation hospitals, skilled nursing facilities, community health centers, individual and group physician practices, managed-care organizations, home health agencies, outpatient laboratories, physical therapy care sites, chiropractors, alternative medicine providers, and others. Major hospitals such as Brigham and Women's in Boston or Mount Sinai in New York City fall into this category, as do health maintenance organizations (HMOs) such as Oxford, and visiting nurse associations (VNAs). In recent years direct care providers have begun focusing on specific populations, such as cancer centers or women's health centers.

Services Supporting Provision of Care

This is somewhat of a catchall for many other aspects of the health-care field, including research organizations, outreach, education, and advocacy groups. Many of the research, outreach, and advocacy organizations are focused on a specific disease or condition, such as the American Heart Association and the American Cancer Society.

Insurance Providers

Insurers such as Blue Cross/Blue Shield also fall into the field of health care. Although they do not provide care to patients, they are responsible for billing, coverage, and other administrative aspects of care. Billing and collections and other technology-based services are critical to this type of health-care organization.

Public Health

Also considered part of the public sector, public health focuses on health at the population level (as opposed to the individual level) and has grown rapidly with the increased recognition of the underlying determinants of good health. Public health organizations typically address issues such as prenatal care, community outreach, immunizations, drug and tobacco use, water and food safety, and disease control. Their programs typically target very broad populations and may have goals of either direct service or public awareness or both. Specific agencies include departments of public health, divisions of human services, Medicaid programs, and Centers for Disease Control at the local, state, and/or federal levels.

Medical Supply, Device, and Pharmaceutical Manufacturers

These players make up a large part of the health-care industry. Such companies are most often profit-making vehicles rather than social enterprises. However, many do play a strong role in social enterprise through donations of goods and services to specific populations, especially overseas.

Hot Topics

Widening Gaps in Insurance Coverage. One of the biggest issues regarding health care in the United States is the fact that approximately forty million Americans do not have health insurance. In fact, the United States is the only industrialized nation that does not have a comprehensive health-care system for all citizens. This is despite the fact that this country spends more than 14 percent of its gross domestic product (GDP) on health care, a greater percentage than any other country in the world. (The comparable figure for Canada is about 9.5 percent and for Japan about 6.5 percent.)

Focus on Prevention. As managed care has grown and the entire industry faces cost-containment pressures, providers have begun to emphasize preventive care. A focus on prevention has been shown to save significant long-term system costs, since the cost of preventive care (for example, regular checkups) is much lower than the cost of emergency care or other intensive intervention.

Care for the Poor. With relentlessly increasing health-care costs and fewer people with sufficient resources to pay for even basic health-care services, the appropriate role of for-profit hospitals, insurers, and managed-care organizations in sharing the costs of care for the poor and uninsured is being hotly debated in each state. Most of these patients eventually qualify for Medicaid or "free-care" status. Medicare and Medicaid were the subject of tremendous political reform controversy in the late 1990s.

The Growth of Managed Care. Managed-care penetration has proliferated in the United States, with some states (including California, Massachusetts, and Minnesota) much more managed-care-saturated than others. Despite growing acceptance, there remains constant tension between quality and cost control in many managed-care organizations.

Growth of Investor-Owned Health Care. For-profit, investor-owned health-care systems are growing in number and in market share. While there are several controversies about the rise in for-profit health care (such as the Columbia/HCA acquisition and rationalization spree), the more positive side of the coin notes that investor-owned institutions force nonprofits to increase efficiency and adopt a more market-driven/customer-driven approach.

"Rationing" of Care. As technology and research capabilities continue to grow exponentially—and potentially outstrip the country's ability to finance such advancements—rationing of health care has become a hotly debated potential solution. This carries weighty implications for sustainable equity of U.S. health-care policy.

Access to Care in Developing Countries. Outside the United States, a continuing important topic is access to health-care services—both preventive and therapeutic—in developing countries. For instance, more than one million children die every year from measles, the vast majority of whom would otherwise live given access to immunization and adequate nutrition. In addition to child mortality and morbidity, other global "hot topics" include high rates of maternal mortality associated with childbirth in many developing countries; access to family planning services; and the rise in smoking rates (with attendant adverse health and financial consequences) in many developing countries.

Roles for MBAs

MBAs can affect the way that health-care resources are allocated in society, in both private and public settings and in both for-profit and nonprofit enterprises. Tremendous pressure is bearing upon all aspects of health care (prevention, treatment, research, and education) to maximize outputs with the smallest overall cost to society. At the same time, competition is increasing, and many health-care organizations are exploring the use of traditional business practices to enhance their long-term survival. Many MBAs manage health-care facilities (a business manager role) or work in strategic planning or other senior management roles in large health-care organizations, which are complex businesses like many others (see profile of Priscilla Cohen in this chapter). In fact, as medicine becomes more of a professional business with serious cost concerns, many physicians are returning to school for business training. The trend toward investor-owned health-care organizations also brings an increasing demand for MBAs, especially MBA/MDs (doctor of medicine) and/or MBA/MPHs (master of public health).

For additional resources and addresses of health-care organizations, see the Resource Road Map.

PRISCILLA COHEN

Hospital management and public-private partnerships

Priscilla Cohen (Harvard Business School, MBA 1988) has worked in government relations, investment banking, health care, education, consulting, low-income housing, child care, and various other aspects of social enterprise. But her career to date has had a consistent unifying theme: "I have been fascinated by the intersection between the various sectors—business, government, and community."

After graduating from Williams College in 1982, Cohen won a Coro Fellowship, a one-year program designed to expose future leaders to multiple sectors that influence public policy. "I worked on a political campaign, with a labor group, in a business, in a community organization—it was an amazing year of experiences. During that year I decided I wanted to create public-private partnerships to address issues of importance to the community. But here I was, a classics major who knew nothing about the business half of the equation." So Cohen went to Morgan Stanley (now Morgan Stanley Dean Witter & Co.), where she spent her first year in corporate finance. "Then an opportunity arose to work in government relations, and to learn more about the role that businesses play in the political process. It was a fascinating perspective."

After her Morgan Stanley experience and a year on a Rotary scholarship in Italy, Cohen landed at HBS. "I became very involved in the Nonprofit Management Club (predecessor of the Social Enterprise Club). It was a good way to meet people with shared values." Over the summer between years of business school, Cohen worked with the Boston Housing Partnership. "I developed and presented a production plan for 1,000 units of low-income housing. I did a lot of community and financial analysis and helped think through how groups of community development corporations (CDCs) could access more government funds if they packaged their development plans than if they worked alone."

During her second year of business school, Cohen worked on a field study with Bright Horizons, a for-profit day-care provider. "Bright Horizons was an interesting opportunity both because the founders (Linda Mason and Roger Brown) were such dynamic, committed individuals and because of the intersection between business and child care that they were creating." After graduation, Cohen joined McKinsey & Company, where she "was fortunate to work on two pro-bono projects in addition to a range of projects for private companies. I designed a strategy for the government to improve low-income housing initiatives, and I also worked with a major teaching hospital in New York. I learned a tremendous amount and worked with bright, talented, and fun people. But after two years I decided that I wanted to work in nonprofit full-time, and I began to look for another job."

After working with the teaching hospital through McKinsey, Cohen decided to continue learning about the health-care field. "I chose to work at Deaconess Hospital, an academic hospital [in Boston] that at the time was in a vulnerable position. But it had also just brought in a committed and visionary new CEO (Dick Gaintner), and I saw the potential for great improvement in the organization." Cohen spent two years as assistant to the COO, working primarily on continuous quality improvement initiatives, but spending some of her time developing new clinical initiatives for the hospital.

"Then a series of external pressures forced the hospital to think more seriously about community outreach. In fact, to gain approval for a new hospital building, Deaconess had to commit to spend $2.6 million on commu-

"Life is short, and at the end of the day you have to feel that you've done something worthwhile. I do."

nity initiatives. Plus, the new leadership was committed to the vision of greater community involvement. So I accepted the challenge to lead the emerging external relations department." Cohen's major responsibilities were to develop a mission and strategy for the new department and, based on that mission, to determine community needs, develop programs to meet those needs, and measure the impact of the programs once they were implemented. "One of my favorite projects was a mall-based heart center we developed in partnership with a health center in Roxbury. The center provided outreach and on-site diagnosis, and included a heavy emphasis on prevention." Part of the senior management team, Cohen helped develop the Pathway Health Network of five hospitals (of which Deaconess was one). "I began to manage the community programs across the network, with the goal of differentiating us as the hospital network truly committed to community health improvement."

During this time, Cohen had become increasingly involved in the community as a member of the board of Citizen Schools, chair of the Cambridge-Ellis school board, and a core member of the planning group for New Profit Inc. At Deaconess she developed a program to support Citizen Schools with a combination of grant funding and employee time off to teach in the Citizen Schools program. (Citizen Schools runs after-school and summer programs for children nine to fourteen.)

After seven years at Deaconess, Cohen was ready for a change, and became a philanthropic consultant working primarily in education—still thinking about how to engage community stakeholders in public-private partnerships. "There is no one path for everyone. I have done many different things, but all related to partnerships among the sectors. I feel lucky that I have had so many great opportunities to learn and to contribute. Life is short, and at the end of the day you have to feel that you've done something worthwhile. I do."

International Aid and Economic Development

Overview

International development refers to both political and economic development of nations around the world. The field can be defined to include relief/aid to developing nations as well as sustainable economic development. According to the University of Sussex in the United Kingdom, "development is about helping communities help themselves." The practice of development evolves constantly to respond to changes in the world economy (such as the Asian financial crisis of 1998).

Development roles are played by governments, multilateral institutions (collaborations of multiple governments), and a broad spectrum of nongovernment organizations (NGOs), which can be national or international, secular or religiously affiliated. The activities of international aid and development organizations range from providing funds, to advising developing nations on public policy, to providing direct relief and development services, to political advocacy. Areas of development range from disaster relief to refugee protection, assistance, and resettlement; to long-term sustainable economic development; to education or public health. Many international organizations and NGOs are headquartered in the United States (primarily New York or Washington, D.C.), London, or Geneva. However, there are also many NGOs in developing countries themselves, and most international organizations have field offices in addition to headquarters.

Subdivisions

Multilateral Development Organizations

These include government-funded official organizations such as the World Bank, the International Monetary Fund, and the United Nations. Multilateral development organizations generally provide loans and/or grants to governments of developing countries (and sometimes to private sector organizations in those countries) to be used for economic development activities, such as the development of transportation infrastructure or education systems when funds are not available from the national government or private sector.

Relief Organizations

Thousands of international organizations assist developing nations by directly providing aid and relief services, either on an ongoing basis or in response to an emergency or disaster such as a major earthquake, famine, or war. They include government organizations and nonprofit NGOs and range in size from a skeletal staff to large international bodies. Large relief organizations include the Red Cross, CARE, and Population Services International.

International Microfinance Organizations

Organizations such as ACCION International and Women's World Banking are private, nonprofit organizations that provide low-cost financing to small businesses and entrepreneurs in underdeveloped nations around the world to assist in the sustainable economic development of those nations. Microfinance organizations are often intermediaries that channel funds to underserved communities that are difficult for large multilateral organizations to reach.

Think Tanks

Experts in development and academics often act as advisors to NGOs and governments. A few examples of international development think tanks are The Brookings Institute, the Heritage Foundation, and the Center for Strategic and International Studies.

Private Sector Consultants

Consultants play a similar role to think tanks, but on a more individual basis, serving as economic or technical advisors to international development organizations. For example, Harvard Professor Jeffrey Sachs is a well-known international development consultant.

Foundations

International foundations such as the Ford Foundation or the Soros Foundation hire program managers for their international funding programs. As in think tanks, employees of these foundations are usually experts on a specific area within the international development field.

Advocacy Organizations

Several organizations focus on advocacy rather than direct aid or service provision. Their goal is to keep government and public attention focused on the importance of providing adequate support to developing nations and respecting core values such as political freedom, human rights, or protection of the environment during periods of economic expansion. Such organizations include Amnesty International and InterAction.

Hot Topics

Decentralization of Development Operations. In the past, many organizations based most staff at headquarters, isolated from the groups they served. A recent shift toward decentralization has put more people in the field working more closely with their "clients" in the developing nations.

Institutional Capacity Building. Building on the quote about "teaching a man to fish rather than giving him a meal," international economic development organizations focus on "capacity building," which involves the transfer of skills from developed to developing countries rather than the transfer of resources alone (for example, food or clothing donations).

Expanding Role of the Private Sector. In the past, individual governments and multilateral organizations funded the majority of development in developing nations. However, these organizations are now encouraging the private sector to undertake more economic development activities. For example, an organization that might have funded the development of a toll road in the past would encourage the private sector to do so instead.

Growth of Microfinance and Encouraging Entrepreneurship. In a similar vein, the field of international development has witnessed a rise in microfinance—making capital available to entrepreneurs in developing nations, including nations such as Thailand that are more developed than the traditional recipients of international aid. The belief driving this growth is that groups such as women, poor communities, and rural residents have the potential to contribute to real economic development growth but are often limited by lack of capital from traditional sources.

Roles for MBAs

In international development fieldwork, specialized skills and qualifications are particularly important. Without a medical background, for instance, it will be very difficult to find fieldwork in medical relief. Groups working in unstable areas try to remain very thinly staffed and will be unlikely to have a place for anyone without the specialization they need. For refugee work, a background in engineering is useful. Think about what specialized skills you may have learned—be they teaching, accounting, even sports coaching—and how these skills might be useful to the sort of organizations you are targeting.

Typical overseas opportunities fall into the following categories:

- Advisory: economists, business experts, academics

- Teaching and health

- Technical: agriculturists, water engineers

- Executive: administrators, planners

MBAs can look for opportunities in an advisory role as a business expert, or in an executive/administrative role. Keep in mind, however, that more senior-level jobs as business experts often require significant field experience, as do many of the "executive" type of posts. At headquarters, however, opportunities for professional managers continue to grow. Organizations like Oxfam America are increasingly trying to professionalize their staffs, which presents excellent opportunities for MBAs.

If you are looking for a job in a developing country rather than in the United States, you have to be committed to living in a developing country, which can be a bit of a shock for those who have always lived in developed countries. Think hard about the lifestyle, possible health risks, and cultural isolation before you contract to spend two years in a place like Benin, for example.

Many organizations do not provide training. You might want to consider a summer position, both to bolster your credentials and to get your feet wet. Almost all organizations have managerial and administrative positions in the United States that contribute significantly to the group's work. Landing a job in international development can be particularly challenging if you are looking to work outside your home country. Getting experience "in the field" can be critical if you are looking for a permanent post abroad, and a summer job can be a great venue for this sort of experience. Many organizations, however, prefer or require that the staff of their field offices be locals, so the summer job search can be tough. Many religious groups sponsor organizations that work in relief and development. Another option is to work domestically in development, in rural areas or in urban communities, to gain field experience before seeking international opportunities.

The World Bank, the International Finance Corporation, regional development banks (such as the Asian Development Bank), and other government-run entities offer international opportunities. Many of these organizations have structured programs and hire through a regular, well-defined process. The downside is that these organizations may also have a more regimented promotion process and bureaucratic environment than other international development organizations.

For additional resources and addresses of international aid and economic development organizations, see the Resource Road Map.

NANCY BARRY

Blazing a trail in international economic development

Since graduating from business school in 1975, Nancy Barry has been a trailblazer in the field of international economic development, with a particular focus on microfinance. As president of Women's World Banking (WWB), a nonprofit global financial institution providing services to low-income women entrepreneurs, Barry is an excellent role model for business students with an interest in economic development. From the time she became WWB's president in 1990, she has increased its capital base sixfold, and WWB affiliates have dramatically increased their annual lending portfolios.

Barry came to WWB to continue a highly distinguished career in economic development. Before business school, Barry spent two years in Peru working on small- and medium-sized industry development. After completing her MBA, Barry went to work for the World Bank, a $20-billion multilateral development agency in Washington, D.C. During a highly successful fifteen-year tenure at the bank, she pioneered a lending program to small- and medium-sized enterprises (SMEs) in developing countries. Previously, the bank had focused on large companies, leaving SMEs without access to capital. Her program eventually grew to represent about a third of the bank's lending through financial intermediaries, or about $2.2 billion.

While at the World Bank, Barry began working informally with WWB, which was born out of the 1975 United Nations Conference marking the "Decade for Women." Because she believed strongly in WWB's mission to provide poor women with access to capital and training to run small businesses, Barry agreed in 1981 to serve as a trustee and eventually as vice chairperson. Ultimately, Barry left her prestigious position as division chief of industrial development at the World Bank to take on the task of building WWB into a sustainable, formidable organization. "At a certain point

"We also look for someone interested in and committed to development, but with experience in banking or finance, if possible, and fluent in other languages."

you have to put your body and spirit where your mouth is," Barry says, recalling her risky move from the plush offices of the World Bank to the struggling NGO.

"Although it was a big change to move from an organization and position where I was surrounded by abundant administrative support . . . I very much believe in what WWB stands for and in the wisdom of a highly decentralized organization. I believe that women in most countries in which we work are the most dynamic economic agents and the most forgotten resource."

WWB's mission is to expand the economic participation of low-income women entrepreneurs by opening access to finance, information, and markets. WWB has a core network of approximately fifty affiliate organizations based in thirty-nine countries in Africa, Asia, Latin America, Europe, and North America. The local affiliates are themselves led by prominent local finance and business women leaders, who provide lending, savings, and business development services to hundreds of thousands of low-income women entrepreneurs. Barry believes the local chapters are WWB's greatest assets, since they keep WWB close to the ground and to the ultimate clients—the borrowers. Her philosophy is to keep WWB as decentralized as possible, using the New York headquarters primarily as a resource for the affiliates and as a source of training. Many of the affiliates are now economically self-sufficient.

"It takes a certain kind of person to thrive in the WWB environment—someone entrepreneurial, yet sensitive to the multicultural issues that we work with on a day-to-day basis. We also look for someone interested in and committed to development, but with experience in banking or finance, if possible, and fluent in other languages," she says.

MICHAEL CHU

From board member to CEO: International microfinance at ACCION

Michael Chu (Harvard Business School, MBA 1976), now president and CEO of ACCION International, made the decision to work full-time for a nonprofit after an extremely successful career in business. After business school, he went to work for the Boston Consulting Group. He left BCG three years later to take a position as assistant to the president at City Investing Company, a large, diversified, multinational conglomerate. From assistant to the president, he was promoted to vice president and eventually CFO of City Investment International, a corporate officer on the manufacturing side of the business. In 1984, Chu took part in a management leveraged buyout (LBO) of the manufacturing group, during which he worked with Kohlberg, Kravis and Roberts (KKR, a well-known leveraged-buyout firm). Chu became senior vice president and CFO of the new company formed for the buyout, and in 1989, KKR invited him to join the group. He stayed with KKR until 1993.

Chu first became involved with ACCION International, a nonprofit organization that fights poverty through microlending and one of the world's leading microfinance organizations, as a board member in 1988. "The guy that gave me my first job ever was on the board of ACCION International, and he recruited me onto the board." Over time, Chu found himself increasingly involved: "I got really interested in what ACCION was doing, developing microfinance into a viable economic activity. They were on the threshold of organizing world capital markets to alleviate poverty." In 1993, he left KKR to join ACCION full-time and was named president in 1994.

Moving from the world of finance to the nonprofit sector brought both tremendous rewards and frustrations. "The best thing is the human dimension of what we're doing. Our ultimate mission is to roll back poverty in the world to affect human life on a massive scale.

"I have been very lucky in my professional career. I have been able to do successfully what had never been done before and to challenge the accepted definition of what is possible. There have been great crises in ACCION's work. Some of the challenges have been as tough as any I have faced in my business career." For example, "many of the traditional funding sources for nonprofits work contrary to how markets work, which is frustrating for nonprofits geared towards performance."

According to Chu, MBAs have important skills to offer the nonprofit world. "Harnessing the skills honed at business school can have tremendous social and economic development impact." However, he points out that entering the social enterprise world directly after graduation is not necessarily the right choice for everyone, despite those skills. "When to do it is the difficult question. I wouldn't have brought the same skills if I had come straight from business school, but ACCION wouldn't exist as it is today if it weren't for colleagues of mine who were plugging away instead of doing LBOs."

"I didn't leave for the nonprofit sector; I left for ACCION."

"The challenge is to find nonprofits that can really use newly minted MBAs to their full potential. It might be the kiss of death for a nonprofit to take someone with ideals and enthusiasm from business school, who after three years becomes extremely frustrated and completely cynical about the nonprofit world."

"At ACCION we tell people if you want to really work hard and be totally committed you will be grossly underpaid but doing something that really matters. However, this message is not that healthy. We need to move to a level where the disparity isn't that high. On the other hand, if you want Wall Street compensation, go to Wall Street. But if the nonprofit world wants to attract and retain quality, it must create situations to attract quality and to attract a good professional base." That means reasonable salaries. "The nonprofit road is not for those who are risk-averse or for those who value the definitions of others greatly. You have to be a lot more independent in your self-conception. Some people can find great comfort in saying, 'I'm a partner at Goldman Sachs.' People who come over to 'the other side' are people who don't give a hoot for that sort of perception.

It requires a tolerance and a like for things that may be controversial."

"If someone asked me if they should wait to get into the nonprofit sector until after making a gazillion bucks on Wall Street, I would say that that's a terrific combination—the absolute luxury of doing something you really love. Helping people brings out the best in people. Sometimes on Wall Street you see the worst of people. It's really a luxury, doing something you love and not worrying about the mortgage. But it's irrelevant to say which road to take because nothing is for certain. Many people on Wall Street think of doing something else but never do, and quite a few look back and regret it even though they have a tremendous sum of money."

Chu cautions about the importance of finding an opportunity about which you are passionate: "I never thought about working in the nonprofit sector until I was exposed to ACCION. I would have never left KKR, which in addition to being obscenely well-compensated was also tremendously intellectually challenging. I didn't leave for the nonprofit sector; I left for ACCION. People should not go into nonprofit work without finding an opportunity that interests and challenges them, just like someone shouldn't go to any investment bank on Wall Street."

Chu made some unconventional choices in the course of his career. His final comment? "One resource that is absolutely precious and finite is time—use it well."

Social Services

Overview

Social service organizations (SSOs), broadly defined, are organizations that provide one or more services directly to individuals in need. SSOs range from lone-volunteer efforts to multimillion-dollar organizations. Most typical "charities" fall into this category (such as soup kitchens, youth development programs, or support services for the elderly).

Three major dimensions differentiate SSOs.

- The first is client scope. SSOs range geographically from serving a single neighborhood (for example, community-based organizations) to serving the entire world (for example, the Red Cross). The organization may also focus on a particular segment of clients based on age, ethnicity, gender, income, or other demographic.

- The second is service scope. Some SSOs will focus on a single service (such as drug rehabilitation); others on a set of related services (a job training program for youth might also provide GED classes). Multiservice agencies may become one-stop shops for clients.

- The third is resources. Resource differences strongly influence the nature of an SSO. A primarily volunteer-driven organization will feel very different from one staffed mostly by professional social workers. Likewise, the mix of public, private, endowment, and in-

come-generated funding will affect the demands on the organization's programs.

The social service subsector is huge, and there is significant overlap between SSO activities and those outlined in other subsectors of this guide, including education, health care, and economic development. This section outlines ten subdivisions of the social service field.

Subdivisions

Umbrella Organizations

Umbrella organizations include the United Way, United Jewish Appeal, and Catholic Charities, among others. These organizations fund and support other SSOs and may also provide their own services. There are also affinity groups (or coalitions) of SSOs such as United Neighborhood Houses, the umbrella organization for New York City's settlement houses. Such organizations usually unite individual SSOs around common issues, and often serve an advocacy or coordination role. If you're looking for an entrée into the social services sector in a given area, starting with one of these umbrella organizations and discussing its grantee list with them might be a place to start.

Aging

In the early twenty-first century the U.S. population over the age of sixty-five will soar as the baby boomers hit retirement age, and the elderly population reaches 20 percent (versus 13 percent in 1998). In addition, the aging population itself is aging: the U.S. Bureau of the Census estimates that between 1995 and 2010, the population over age eighty-four is expected to grow by 56 percent, as compared with 13 percent for the population aged sixty-five to eighty-four. As our society ages, social service organizations are taking responsibility for caring for the older population.

The National Council on Aging provides a categorized list of elderly services: adult day-care services, advocacy, case management, elder abuse services, emergency response systems, financial assistance/planning, food and nutrition services, health services, home health visits, hospice care, housing services (including nursing homes), intergenerational programs, and senior centers.

AIDS Treatment, Prevention, and Advocacy

The facts on AIDS are frightening. According to a report by the Centers for Disease Control, as of December 1997, 641,086 Americans have been reported as having AIDS. As new treatments have extended the healthy lifespan of many people with AIDS, its prevalence has continued to increase, leading to the development of a social service industry to meet the needs of this population, as well as their friends and families. Organizations fall into three main groups: treatment, prevention, and advocacy. Many organizations take on two or all three of these activities.

Alcohol and Substance Abuse Treatment

Many small organizations and self-help groups have emerged across the country to help people overcome addictions to alcohol and other substances. These small organizations exist side-by-side with large treatment centers and hospital-run programs. Programs may be funded by government, donations, patients, or a mix of all three. In addition, counselors in private practice may run their own therapy groups or offer one-on-one counseling to addicts. The field is undergoing change now as managed care begins to pinch payment to the larger centers, and advances in research are making it possible to evaluate the efficacy of various types of treatment.

Alcohol and substance abuse professionals draw a distinction between residential care, in which the patient lives at the treatment center for thirty days or more, and outpatient care, in which the patient stays at home but comes regularly for treatment.

Children and Youth

According to the Carnegie Corporation's report, *Starting Points,* a staggering number of our nation's children are at risk due to inadequate prenatal care, isolated parents, substandard child care, poverty, inadequate health care, and insufficient attention.

Many social service organizations covered elsewhere in this guide provide services to children and youth. For example, children's health services are provided by health service organizations and hospitals; and of course the education system is the nexus for an array of services to young people, both for-profit and nonprofit.

- *Child care.* Every day, thirteen million preschoolers (about three in five children) are in some form of child care. The lack of affordable child care is especially pressing in poor communities. Federal, state, and local assistance exists for families who cannot afford child care, but currently only one in ten eligible children receive assistance. According to the Children's Defense Fund, categories of child care can be defined by the setting in which the care is delivered: child-care centers; family/home-based child care (provided by someone other than the child's family); in-home caregivers (such as nannies); and relative care. Several resource and referral organizations help parents find care in their area.

- *Literacy/school readiness programs.* School readiness is a combination of cognitive development (including literacy), social/emotional development, health status, and supportive family environment. There is significant overlap between school readiness and other subcategories of the zero- to six-year-old segment of the continuum. Literacy is a distinct category of school readiness that is both critical and fairly easy to address with sufficient commitment to the goal. Educational experts note that until third grade, children learn to read. Beginning in third grade, children read to learn. With the America Reads program sponsored by the federal government, this issue received increasing attention in the late 1990s, but much work remains to ensure that all children enter third grade able to read and ready to learn.

- *Advocacy organizations.* Since children cannot vote, advocacy organizations are important vehicles to protect their treatment in the political and legal system. For example, the Children's Defense Fund's mission is to provide "a strong, effective voice for all the children of America who cannot vote, lobby, or speak for themselves."

- *Youth education, after-school, and summer programs.* These programs (also discussed in the education section) include activities such as arts education or sports. Nonprofit organizations in the field include the National Foundation for Teaching Entrepreneurship (NFTE) and mentoring programs such as Management Leadership for Tomorrow (see Rice profile in this chapter). Summer programs include organizations such as Summerbridge, which provides educational activities, or day camps and overnight camps sponsored by organizations such as the YMCA.

- *Youth economic development programs* such as Youthbuild offer job training, education, counseling, and leadership development opportunities to unemployed and out-of-school young adults. Youthbuild trains young adults through the construction and rehabilitation of affordable housing in their own communities. Many graduates go on to construction-related jobs or college. Alumni receive post-program counseling. The buildings that are rehabilitated or constructed during the program are usually owned and managed by community-based organizations as permanent low-income housing.

Family Support Services

Family support services help families create a healthy home environment and are often focused on parenting decisions and skills.

- *Family planning.* Teen pregnancy and parenting services are an important subgroup of family planning. For example, Planned Parenthood is a national network of clinics that provide sexuality education, abortion, adolescent services, early pregnancy detection, and voluntary sterilization. They also advocate for reproductive freedom, universal access to services, first amendment rights, patients' rights, population control, and women's rights.

- *Home visiting programs.* Many new parents are overwhelmed by the major responsibility that descends upon them when they bring home their baby for the first time. Home visiting services have been shown to help parents adjust, to help them learn how to care for their child, and to significantly decrease the likelihood of child abuse and/or neglect. Home visiting is one of the services offered by organizations such as the Massachusetts Children's Trust Fund and the Society for Prevention of Cruelty to Children.

- *Adoption/foster care organizations.* Adoption and foster care are often a function of the public sector and the legal system, though many private organizations exist as well. Types of adoption agencies include referral services, local public agencies, licensed private adoption agencies, adoptive parent support groups, and post-adoption services such as support groups for adopted adults and birth relatives. Many agencies specialize in adoptions of children from specific international regions (by parents in the United States).

Domestic Violence Support

This broad category covers organizations involved in prevention, education, intervention, and legal aid. Organizations may include one or more of the following:

- Shelters that provide safety for victims of abuse, as well as protection of the residents' identities to allow them to hide from their abusers.

- Counseling to help victims recover from the abuse they suffered.

- Group homes for abused or neglected children that provide education, counseling, and other services.

- Assistance for victims of spousal abuse who are looking for new housing and/or a new job.

- Parenting classes and other services to families identified by other agencies as "at risk" of becoming abusive.

- Hotlines for reporting abuse, or to assist victims looking for services in their communities.

- Publicity departments that educate communities on issues of abuse and domestic violence.

- Researchers who study patterns of abuse and violence to determine the best strategies for intervention.

Food Security/Hunger

According to the antihunger organization Share Our Strength, thirty-five million Americans are hungry or at risk of hunger. During 1997, requests for emergency food assistance rose by 16 percent—and it is estimated that 19 percent of these requests went unmet. Beyond antipoverty efforts covered elsewhere in this guide, there are three basic approaches to fighting hunger: food assistance, nutrition, and advocacy.

- *Food Assistance* programs include food banks, which donate and distribute prepared meals and groceries; food rescue programs, which capture food from producers, grocers, and restaurants that would otherwise be wasted; and community gardens, farmers' markets, and gleaning projects, which seek alternative food sources. Food assistance programs must address both the supply side (food banks) and distribution system (food pantries, soup kitchens, social service agencies).

- *Growth and Nutrition* organizations recognize that the problem is often not just having enough food, but also ensuring adequate nutrition. This is especially important for children as they grow and develop. Nutrition efforts involve treating malnourished children and providing education to families and those who feed them. For example, Share Our Strength's Operation Frontline coordinates and trains volunteer chefs to teach classes for six weeks on nutrition, healthy cooking, and food budgeting to individuals at risk of hunger and malnutrition.

- *Advocacy organizations* attempt to influence public policy on hunger and its causes. Examples include Bread for the World and Oxfam America.

Homelessness

The National Alliance to End Homelessness estimates that 750,000 Americans are homeless on any given night, and between 1.3 and 2 million people experience homelessness each year. People become homeless for many reasons, but many experts agree that poverty, an inadequate supply of affordable housing, and a lack of social services all contribute significantly to the problem.

Many homeless people suffer from other disabilities—such as mental illness, drug or alcohol abuse, illness, HIV/AIDS, or a physical disability. Many have had experience in the criminal justice system, which makes it difficult for them to find employment. Finally, there is a significant population of homeless families with its own set of special needs.

Organizations across the country provide a range of services to help move homeless people towards decent housing and independent living. Some of those services include:

- Outreach and provision of medical help to those on the street

- Drop-in centers that provide referral to other services

- Emergency shelter

- Detoxification, drug and alcohol treatment

- Mental health services

- Legal services

- Job training and education

- Referral to housing

- Permanent housing with supportive services

Multiservice Organizations

Many organizations do not fit into any one category and in fact provide a broad offering of services covering many if not all of the topics addressed in this social service section. Such multiservice organizations include settlement houses, neighborhood houses, YMCAs/YWCAs, community centers, and other organizations.

Hot Topics

Increased Competition for Government Resources. Since the War on Poverty in the 1960s—and probably since the New Deal—government funding has been the bread and butter of SSOs in the United States. Indeed, for better or for worse, government contracts have in the past "crowded out" many traditional philanthropic activities. While these contracts have represented a steady income stream for decades for many SSOs, they have also left them subject to political changes. Block grants to the states and decreased funding overall in the 1990s have hurt many nonprofits, especially those that were dependent on only a few grants. Changes in government funding have affected segments of the social services industry differently. For instance, segments with greater political support, like the elderly and child care, have been protected from cutbacks relative to more vulnerable programs such as those serving immigrants or adolescents.

Welfare and Immigration Reform. Welfare reform (cutbacks) has increased the needs of many poor people and thus increased the burden on the SSOs who serve them. It has also increased the need for job training and job creation programs. Immigration reform has created a new need for legal services and citizenship training and has increased the vulnerability of immigrants in society. Welfare reform has also created a dilemma for many SSOs: Should they use the services of welfare recipients in mandatory welfare-to-work programs? While some argue that SSOs can give more meaningful job experiences to welfare workers (and get the benefits of free help), others argue that their moral and political opposition to the program itself outweighs any potential benefit.

Changing Demographics. Societal trends also affect social service organizations and their clients. SSOs face the challenges of an aging society, greater income disparities between rich and poor, the impact of technology and the "knowledge economy" on employability, and increasing risks to health such as AIDS and violent crime.

Outcome Funding and Privatization. Many SSOs are dealing with two major shifts in the way resources are allocated. Outcomes funding is increasingly demanded by foundations who want to see results, not just processes (for example, instead of being held accountable for the number of clients trained, an employment agency might need to demonstrate how many clients held jobs after a certain period of time). Meanwhile, privatization has brought new, for-profit competitors into fields traditionally dominated by nonprofit organizations.

Roles for MBAs

Just as the social service industry is incredibly broad, the range of opportunities for MBAs is broad as well. However, unless you have had significant experience with one of the "content areas" discussed, the value you bring as an MBA is primarily business acumen and functional exper-

tise. Typical MBA roles are in functional areas such as marketing, finance, or strategic planning (if the organization is large enough). Some MBAs take on management responsibility for a program area. MBAs who have demonstrated their capabilities in the organization or in the private sector but with significant volunteer time may move into senior management positions (see profile of Patrick Aitcheson, chapter 2).

As you research SSOs for potential job opportunities, you may want to look to both foundations who fund the program areas you are interested in and umbrella organizations in those areas. Each will be a good source of information about high-quality organizations.

For additional resources and addresses of social service organizations, see the Resource Road Map.

JOHN RICE

Mentoring tomorrow's leaders

Many MBAs volunteer in social sector organizations while working in the corporate sector. Others work for or build their own nonprofit organizations. John Rice (Harvard Business School, MBA 1992) has pursued both of these paths—at once. Rice is the director of marketing, Latin America, for the National Basketball Association (NBA). He is also the founder of Management Leadership for Tomorrow (MLT), an organization created "To increase the number of qualified minority students at major graduate business schools in preparation for leadership positions in corporations, nonprofit organizations, and entrepreneurial ventures." The means to this end is a program that encourages minority MBAs and business leaders to become volunteer mentors for college students.

While in business school, Rice worked with a professor to look at minority student presence at major business schools and minority underrepresentation in leadership positions in the public and private sectors. Through this research and other independent work, several things stimulated Rice's thinking. First, campus research revealed that minority undergraduates in particular lacked career mentors. Second, he became increasingly aware of the large number of minority and nonminority MBA

"It's not about making money first and giving back later. It's about doing what you believe in throughout your life."

graduates who did not have a "user-friendly" vehicle through which to help young people achieve what they themselves had achieved. And third, he had been bothered by how many of his peers said that first they would become successful in their field, and then *later* they would be able to give back.

Rice believed that providing MBAs with a high-impact, "low-ish" time commitment opportunity to help younger minorities would address all three issues, and set out to build a mentoring program—Management Leadership for Tomorrow (MLT). "I felt lucky to have had parents, family, and friends who supported me throughout my life, and access to a fairly strong network in the broader community. I wanted to provide that to others, so I said, 'I'm going to do this' . . . and here I am."

After graduation, Rice went to work for Disney in Orlando, Florida. "If timing had been different, I might have tried to work on MLT full-time. But I had this great opportunity at Disney before I had developed the full concept of MLT, and I felt that getting more experience running a business and developing a larger network while at Disney would actually help get this going." So

Rice built MLT in his spare time, supported by a $10,000 grant from Citibank.

By late 1993 he had hired his first employee, who initially worked out of her home in Atlanta. Together they worked on raising money, researching areas of need, and seeking out potential partners. By the fall of 1994, MLT was "operational," and they began doing campus outreach for mentees, recruiting mentors, and matching the two. As of 1998, MLT had about 150 mentoring pairs, with the goal of expanding into the thousands, and had hired a full-time president. Meanwhile Rice had moved from Disney to the NBA, still working long hours in the corporate sector as his volunteer organization grew.

"I had always wanted to do it all—work in business, run a nonprofit—but it is extremely difficult to do two jobs at once, when you care deeply about them both. I got to the point where I wanted to focus on MLT full-time. So I talked to the NBA and asked for a leave of absence to get MLT to a more solidly grounded point and establish the foundation for aggressive program growth. They were very supportive and gave me three months off to go do it."

Rice's commitment has been driven by a firmly rooted belief that giving back should be a part of life from very early on. "It's not about making money first and giving back later. It's about doing what you believe in throughout your life."

ROSEANN HASSEY

Supporting families

Roseann Hassey (Harvard Business School, MBA 1987) reflects on her unusual career path after a long day at Beech Acres, a family service center in Cincinnati, Ohio. Beech Acres provides counseling and support to parents with an historical focus on low-income, "at-risk" families. Now vice president of the organization, Hassey has worked with the CEO to achieve dramatic growth over the past five years. She describes herself as head of "marketing and new product development" for this innovative social enterprise.

"I was always drawn to the idea of doing well while also doing good."

By defining who the customers are and then reorganizing the organization to better serve them, Hassey has been instrumental in charting a new strategy for the organization. When she arrived at Beech Acres, it had an endowment of $40 million and an annual budget of $4 million. By 1999, the endowment had reached over $60 million and the annual operating budget was $24 million.

Even before business school, Hassey had a feeling that her career would not follow a traditional path. Though she had spent two years after college working in brand management for Procter & Gamble, she wanted to contribute directly to the social sector. "I was always drawn to the idea of doing well while also doing good," she says.

So Hassey applied to both the Kennedy School of Government and the Harvard Business School. She then sought advice from John MacArthur, then dean of the Business School. He told her that the Business School aimed to train community leaders, not just business leaders. He advised her to come to HBS, get a few years of experience in the for-profit world to sharpen her business skills, and then make the leap into the nonprofit world "as a business leader."

Hassey has never regretted following his advice. Immediately after graduation, she worked for two years in the placement office at HBS. In her spare time, she worked with Elizabeth Glasser (Harvard Business School, MBA 1988) and now-Professor Jeffrey Bradach to found Community Impact, which connected young professionals with volunteer opportunities in Boston. By the time she left, over 350 professionals were actively involved in the program. She still looks back on that experience as "one of the accomplishments I'm most proud of."

Then she returned to the business world, as brand manager and then marketing director for Reebok in Boston. "It was a fun time," she remembers. "We were bigger than Nike back then." Her marketing positions with Reebok and Procter & Gamble prior to earning her MBA taught her to think about strategic problems, she says, and shaped her thinking in ways that would later prove very useful in the nonprofit world. "I learned to be quick on my feet," she remembers, and that "you need to understand the customer or you miss the market."

In 1992, Hassey and her husband decided to move to Cincinnati, and soon their first child was born. A friend of hers who knew that she was looking for her next job encouraged her to meet the CEO of Beech Acres. When she did, Hassey soon realized that the two were a perfect match. The CEO was a business-oriented social worker, and Hassey was a socially minded business person, so they immediately clicked. Because the organization had an endowment, she knew it could afford to invest strategically, unlike many organizations that had to worry about day-to-day cash flow above all else. The CEO and Hassey shared a vision of expanding their services to all families in the community, not only the most "at risk." So she signed on to help make that vision a reality.

Over the past few years Beech Acres has started a managed-care company for Greater Cincinnati's neediest children and has launched a new information technology system that helps Beech Acres staff manage and measure their results. Hassey also played a key role in reorganizing Beech Acres into three business units focusing on intensive services, prevention, and a "new product development" entity called Promoting Healthy Families.

"I count my blessings every day that I actually get paid to do such meaningful work."

Even more important, she finds her work rewarding. "Even though I cut my salary in half to do the work I do, I find the work extremely fulfilling and, in fact, I count my blessings every day that I actually get *paid* to do such meaningful work." In addition, because her skills and background are relatively unique, she has been able to negotiate a flexible work schedule to be with her three young children while continuing to maintain a significant leadership position at work.

Social Purpose Businesses

Overview

A social purpose business is a for-profit business venture created to promote social change through profitable enterprise ("business for a cause"). As described in the introduction, social purpose businesses are in some ways a product of the intersection of the three traditional sectors—public, private, and nonprofit. Social purpose businesses have two sets of distinguishing characteristics: they have direct or indirect impact on one or more social needs; and they emphasize earned income rather than philanthropy or government subsidy. Social purpose businesses have a "double bottom line"—their goal is to have a direct impact on a social need while generating a profit.

Bill Shore, founder of Share Our Strength and Community Wealth Ventures, talks about generating resources through "profitable enterprise to promote social change," which he calls community wealth. Thus *community wealth,* rather than *shareholder wealth,* is the ultimate goal of a social purpose business, distinguishing it from other for-profit companies.

Social purpose businesses include both business enterprises developed by nonprofits to generate income for the organizations (and sometimes defining them as for-profit subsidiaries) and for-profit organizations created to meet a social need.

Subdivisions

Stand-Alone Social Purpose Businesses

A stand-alone social purpose business is a for-profit entity created to serve a social purpose, and is independent of other organizations. Two examples of social purpose businesses (both founded by HBS graduates) are CitySoft and WorkSource Staffing Partnership, Inc. (see profiles in this chapter). In addition, Juma Ventures—in partnership with Ben & Jerry's—operates scoop shops that involve at-risk youth in all aspects of the business and reinvest profits in employee training and new business development. And Newman's Own, a company founded by actor Paul Newman, donates 100 percent of after-tax profits (from sales of products such as salsa, salad dressing, and organic pretzels) to charity.

Subsidiary Social Purpose Businesses

Subsidiary social purpose businesses are generally started by nonprofits to support their other activities—and are sometimes set up as for-profit subsidiaries of that organization. For example, the Delancey Street Foundation—which provides job training, peer counseling, shelter, food, and other necessities to people trying to overcome problems with crime, drugs, or alcohol—also runs nine for-profit enterprises including a restaurant, a moving company, roller-blade rentals, and seasonal Christmas tree sales—all of which generate profits to sustain the larger organization. In addition, Community Wealth Ventures is a for-profit subsidiary of the nonprofit Share Our Strength (see profile later in this chapter).

Hot Topics

Perceived Conflict with Mission. At times nonprofit organizations face criticism from skeptics who suggest that the revenues produced from a profitable business model may distract the staff from the organization's original mission. For-profit social purpose organizations also are questioned about whether they are truly focused on a so-cial mission or whether they are using that aspect of their business as a tool to drive up profits.

Double Bottom Line. Social purpose organizations are accountable for a "double bottom line"—the financial health of an organization and the health of the communities it serves. This complicates the traditional business model and poses new challenges for social entrepreneurs. Social purpose businesses have to think about the hidden social costs—and benefits—that transcend the easily quantifiable financial accounting for the organization.

The Role of the Social Mission in Sales and Marketing. Though the social mission is an integral part of the social purpose business, it may not be the driving force behind the sales process. Finding a balance between marketing the mission and marketing the specific product or service offering can be challenging at times.

Tax Issues. Tax relief has been a big incentive for charitable giving over the years. Corporate sponsorships, for example, create tax incentives for corporations to support a particular cause. Tax regulations are changing, however, directly affecting corporate participation in many nonprofit partnership situations. In addition, legal and tax issues regarding the income from a social enterprise may have a negative impact on the financial value derived from the activity.

Roles for MBAs

MBAs may find the social purpose business world to be a closer fit with their backgrounds and experience than more traditional nonprofit organizations. Several MBAs have worked in or started up their own social purpose businesses (see profiles later in this chapter). Since most of these enterprises are fairly small and entrepreneurial, the typical role is to be a general manager, product developer, marketing vice president, or president/founder, or to fill another senior functional position. MBAs are also often sought to run business enterprises within larger nonprofit organizations (see profile of Lisa Schorr, director of business enterprise development at the Pine Street Inn, chapter 2).

For additional resources and addresses of social purpose businesses, see the Resource Road Map.

SARAH PERRY

Creating community wealth

Sarah Perry (Harvard Business School, MBA 1995) never truly saw herself as a typical consultant. But for many reasons, she accepted a position with McKinsey & Company in New York after she graduated with a joint degree from HBS and the Kennedy School of Government. Though Perry enjoyed consulting work, she was more interested in combining aspects of the business world with her passion for social change and was looking to find an entrepreneurial environment where she could generate impact. And then one day, she read *Revolution of the Heart,* a book written by Bill Shore, founder of Share Our Strength (a national hunger and poverty relief organization).

Shore's book articulated the need to merge the best of the corporate world with the needs of the nonprofit sector to generate new sources of revenue—through profitable enterprise and partnerships with the for-profit sector rather than through traditional means (grants, donations, etc.). At the time, Shore was starting a new for-profit consulting company, Community Wealth Ventures (CWV), which would provide consulting and technical assistance to nonprofit organizations, foundations, and corporate clients to help them build social enterprise ventures, and to apply a new way of thinking about the social sector. Inspired by his concept, Perry telephoned Shore to arrange a meeting to discuss some of the ideas expressed in the book.

By the meeting's end, Perry had been offered a job as vice president of CWV—an opportunity to help define the emerging world of social enterprise. It was a perfect fit with her interests, background, and skills. She comments, "CWV was exactly what I was looking for. It offered me the chance to work for an innovative and socially responsible start-up company, and to apply my consulting skills to help nonprofits change how they operate." It was an opportunity she could not turn down.

Despite the great new opportunity, the decision to leave McKinsey was not easy. Perry had enjoyed working for a company that offered a great deal of intellectual stimulation and well-structured opportunities for learning. She felt that she was growing her skills and having an impact at high levels within client organizations. And it was "hard to leave an environment like McKinsey, and to give up the prestige, the collegial and rich learning environment, and the security for something very unknown—and to go to an organization that takes multiple sentences to explain." She felt that many of her peers labeled her job as a "nonprofit thing" and with that came a perceived loss of respect as she moved to an organization that others falsely believed was less performance-driven, accountable, and business-minded. Still, she felt that the opportunity to join CWV was worth the trade-offs since "building an enterprise in the social sector and being part of a dynamic start-up was exactly what I wanted to do."

> *"Building an enterprise in the social sector and being part of a dynamic start-up was exactly what I wanted to do."*

Perry found that CWV was an organization well-positioned for the demands of the new social enterprise industry. Many nonprofit organizations needed the management expertise and guidance that CWV could provide, and Perry was in a critical leadership position. As an entrepreneur in a new and fast-growing company she felt even more accountable to develop the business, and she worked long hours to establish herself and her company as a model for success. She was responsible for engaging new clients, building the organization, and working on several projects at once.

As she made the transition from the for-profit world into the nonprofit sector, Perry faced many unexpected challenges. She found herself applying a business model to organizations that didn't understand her language or have the capacity to implement some of her initial recommendations. "I had to shift my mentality to work with nonprofits" she recalls. "In the beginning I wasn't realistic about how nonprofits work." The start-up nature of CWV presented a further challenge. Working under initial budget constraints, CWV was building a business to serve a market that has significant financial constraints of its own.

Perry's career goals are simply stated, but ambitious. "I want to be one of the success stories. I hope to lead or start my own social service organization that achieves self-sufficiency through entrepreneurial activity. I have been a consultant, but I ultimately want to work within an organization, initiating the changes and feeling the direct impact of what I am recommending."

NICK GLEASON

Creating opportunities through the Internet

"Starting a business from scratch is like being shot out of a cannon," says Nick Gleason (Harvard Business School, MBA 1997). "I love it." Now he strives to give others the same thrill with CitySoft Inc., a for-profit company that employs adults from lower-income urban neighborhoods. The company provides high-quality Internet outsourcing services to premier companies. At the same time, CitySoft is committed to hiring and promoting talented, pre-trained Web developers and managers from technologically isolated urban neighborhoods. With its corporate clients and community partners, CitySoft creates opportunities for individuals from isolated urban areas to become active participants in the mainstream, Internet economy.

"I see empowerment and entrepreneurship going together. People get motivated when they are not just a cog in the machine."

CitySoft employees provide a full range of Web services, from database development and integration to graphic design and multimedia. "We are harnessing the high-growth Internet industry to counter the technological isolation and low wages associated with inner-city neighborhoods," says Gleason, who co-founded the Boston-based company. "Web development requires a wide range of skills, and by matching employees to the appropriate challenges, we are able to provide quick, high-quality, competitively priced work," says Gleason.

The impetus for CitySoft stemmed from Gleason's belief that social interests can be compatible with business, a concept that reflects both his family's social activism and his own experience as an entrepreneur. His father was an organizer during the Mississippi Freedom Summer of 1964; his mother teaches literacy and is also a community organizer. Following their lead, Gleason devoted himself to urban development, working for a variety of organizations and agencies before launching a consulting business, Gleason Associates, and then attending business school. "Starting Gleason Associates was the most powerful professional experience of my life," he says. "I found it incredibly exciting, motivating, and empowering. I began to think that entrepreneurship had the potential to create positive opportunities and change in low-income neighborhoods."

This idea continued to percolate while Gleason attended HBS. He started working with two teenagers on Web projects, mostly as an aside, until he took a course on managing product development. Gleason mentioned his project to his professor, Marco Iansiti, who "went through the roof." Iansiti enthusiastically encouraged Gleason to develop his idea and even connected him with his assistant, Jim Picariello, who became Gleason's partner in CitySoft.

In the summer of 1997, CitySoft received a $25,000 start-up grant from the Echoing Green Foundation. For the first six months of operation, the company functioned out of bedrooms, basements, Gleason's car, and the facilities of nonprofit partners. Gleason and Picariello, with the help of two freelance designers from Roxbury, Massachusetts, and ten part-time contractors from inner-city training centers, proceeded to embark on a journey of growth and opportunity in this innovative marriage of social concerns with business interests. They now have office space of their own in Kendall Square in Cambridge.

Since its inception, CitySoft has been featured in a variety of media, including the *Wall Street Journal*, MSNBC, *Swing Magazine,* and CNN. The unique synergy of CitySoft's business strategy and social mission has enabled CitySoft to become a credible Internet start-up company with a growing list of clients including Boston.com, Siemens, Houghton Mifflin, and Stonyfield Farm. As a result, the founders have been grappling with questions such as the optimal level of growth for sustainability and continued success, and how to introduce the discipline required to build CitySoft into a national, competitive organization. Gleason and Picariello have already received several offers to start CitySoft franchises in New York, Chicago, and other cities.

"I see empowerment and entrepreneurship going together," Gleason says. "People get motivated when they are not just a cog in the machine."

Socially Responsible Business/Corporate Community Relations

Overview

Socially responsible businesses try to balance the bottom line with a sense of social mission, or to "do good while doing well." These businesses are characterized by their policies (such as safe environmental practices, child care for employees, etc.) and their activities in the community (for example, relationships with community organizations, and employee volunteer programs). As noted earlier, such organizations include Ben & Jerry's, the Body Shop, Stonyfield Farm, and even large companies such as IBM and Xerox Corporations, who have increasingly emphasized their role as corporate citizens. Interest in social responsibility has been growing rapidly over the years, and organizations such as Business for Social Responsibility and NetImpact have emerged to help guide the development of this field.

To manage their community involvement, most major corporations have a position for community relations (sometimes called government/community relations or corporate contributions manager). The role of a community relations director is to manage the "social investments" or community activities of the corporation. The larger the company, the more likely this will be a full-time, paid position. For example, Timberland's community relations director managed the City Year partnership initiatives as well as multiple other corporate volunteering and community involvement programs. The profile of Nancy Lane, a vice president in government relations at Johnson & Johnson (profiled in this chapter), illustrates the challenges and rewards of working in this field. Though Lane's experience has been extremely positive, this is not necessarily true of her counterparts in all organizations. Some community relations directors have found that at times their activities are very constrained by the interests and direction of the company CEO or board of directors, and they lack the power and latitude to take initiative they have had in other management positions.

In recent years, companies have taken a more innovative approach to involvement in the social sector, as highlighted in a 1998 conference chaired by Professor Kanter, entitled "Business Leadership in the Social Sector." For example, IBM's "Reinventing Education" project leveraged IBM's strengths in information technology to help transform public education.

For additional resources and addresses of socially responsible businesses, see the Resource Road Map.

NANCY LANE

Corporate responsibility to the community

Nancy Lane is a vice president in the government relations department of Johnson & Johnson (J&J). Her responsibilities are focused on community relations; she manages a number of programs that belong to a larger portfolio of J&J community involvement activities. In 1997, J&J gave over $146.3 million to community programs and organizations around the world through a combination of in-kind contributions ($96.9 million) and direct financial support ($49.4 million)—both at the corporate and the operating company levels.

"The J&J Credo says that we have a responsibility to the communities in which we live and work, and we are committed to stay true to our credo. When you are the leading corporation in a small town, and committed to social responsibility, you dedicate a significant portion of your resources to community activities."

> *"I feel very fortunate to be at a company that values what I value. I love my job because I know that I am making a difference in the community."*

One of Lane's primary responsibilities is to manage J&J's Community Health Care Program, a partnership with the National Council of La Raza, Morehouse School of Medicine, and the Johns Hopkins School of Public Health. The program's goal is to "address the health-care needs of the medically under-served," in large part by providing grants "to nonprofit organizations that propose creative and effective ways of promoting health care services." The national program gives two-year, $100,000 grants to six organizations per year, distributed evenly over the two-year period so that J&J maintains a "portfolio" of twelve grantees. Lane gets very involved with grant recipients: "I work with an outside group to help choose the right organizations but work closely with this group to develop an outreach strategy and evaluate the programs we fund. I also visit all of the organizations each year to learn more about what they do."

Lane manages another major program, a business training and development program for directors of Head Start Programs. "When you think of Head Start, you typically think of the teachers and the day-care centers themselves. But behind each program is a director running a business—subcontracting for transportation and food delivery, planning curricula, managing the staff, and so much more. And most of these individuals have worked their way up from the day-care teacher position with a background in education, not management." So J&J developed the Johnson & Johnson Management Fellows Program in collaboration with the Anderson School of Management at the University of California–Los Angeles (UCLA). Selected Head Start directors from around the country participate in a two-week, intensive mini-MBA program at UCLA, paid for by J&J. During the program they learn finance, logistics management, leadership, general management, and other MBA skills. Participants also design a management improvement project (MIP) for their centers, which they review with their bosses during the last few days of the course.

Lane came to her current position after many years in human resources at J&J. "I had always been involved in the community on a personal basis. I have been on the boards of several colleges, including chair of the board of Bennett College (one of two African-American colleges for women in the United States). I have been involved with several museums and other cultural organizations. I have worked with many health-care institutions. When this job was offered to me I was thrilled. It gave me the opportunity to bring my work and my community involvement together."

From J&J's perspective, community relations activities are good for the community and good for the bottom line, in terms of customer and supplier relations, employee relations and productivity, government relations, and more. "We used to call what we do philanthropy, but now we truly think of it as social investment. There is clear business value in what we do." In fact, the former head of the Johnson & Johnson philanthropy department, Curtis Weeden, has recently written a book entitled *Corporate Social Investing* (see Resource Road Map for more information). J&J's community involvement extends well beyond Lane's programs to include a diabetes camp, a Wharton Fellows Program in Management for Nurse Executives, the American Business Collaborative for Quality Dependent Care, International Relief efforts, support for biomedical and other scientific research, and much more (for more information, see J&J's annual report: Social Responsibility in Action Worldwide).

For Lane, the job is extremely rewarding. "You get to meet the people whose lives have been changed by our investment and support. Going to the Head Start graduations is always a thrill." However, the downside is that "there is only a limited amount that we can give. So you see what a difference you can make, and then feel badly when you know that you have to say no to some very worthy organizations."

For MBAs who want to pursue a career in community relations, Lane shares some insights on the path. "It's difficult, because there are so few of these jobs. How one gets there is a combination of good business skills, prior involvement with community organizations, and knowledge of the corporation itself." The third criterion is especially important because corporate giving has become increasingly strategic and tied to the core business of many companies.

At J&J, for example, the process of giving health-care products to organizations around the world requires deep knowledge of the company's manufacturing and distribution operations—and the employee responsible for this segment of community outreach has just that knowledge.

CHAPTER SIX

Resource Road Map

The Resource Road Map is an in-depth bibliography arranged by topic and industry subsector. Among the many resources listed are associations, Web sites, career guides, books, articles, case studies, and organizations.

The organization lists in the road map are by no means exhaustive. Those listed were chosen because they are known as organizations that are well run, fairly large (with some exceptions), and receptive to working with MBAs. For a more complete listing of nonprofit organizations in the United States, see *The National Directory of Nonprofit Organizations* (Rockville, MD: The Taft Group, 1998 (800) 877-8238).

General Nonprofit Resources

Information Sources

- *Chronicle of Philanthropy,* <http://philanthropy.com>

- Contact Center Network, <www.contact.org>

- The Drucker Foundation, <www.drucker.org>

- Gale Research. *The Encyclopedia of Associations and National Organizations.* Detroit, MI: Gale Research Inc. 1998.

- GuideStar, <www.guidestar.org>

- The Independent Sector, <www.indepsec.org>

- The National Council of Nonprofit Associations, <ncna@ncna.org>

- *NonProfit Times,* <www.nptimes.com>

- The Support Center for Nonprofit Management, (415) 541-9000

- The Taft Group. *National Directory of Nonprofit Organizations.* Rockville, MD: The Taft Group, 1998. (800) 877-8238

Nonprofit job listings

- Access: networking in the public interest, <www.communityjobs.org>

- The MBA Nonprofit Connection, (415) 323-9639

- Opportunity NOCs, <www.opnocs.org>

- Net Impact (formerly Students for Responsible Business), <www.net-impact.org>

- <www.idealist.org/career>

- <www.monster.com>

- <www.nonprofitcareer.com>

- <www.nonprofitjobs.org>

Career-Oriented Guidebooks

- Cohen, Lilly, and Dennis R. Young. *Careers for Doers and Dreamers.* New York: The Foundation Center, 1989.

- Cowan, Jessica, ed. *GoodWorks: A Guide to Careers in Social Change.* New York: Barricade/Dembner Books, 1991. (212) 228-8828

- Gardella, Robert. *The Harvard Business School Guide to Finding Your Next Job.* Boston, MA: Harvard Business School Publishing, 2000.

- Hamilton, Leslie, and Robert Tragert. *The 100 Best Nonprofits to Work For.* New York: Beach Brook Productions, 1998.

- Krannich, Ronald L., and Caryl Rae Krannich. *Jobs and Careers with Nonprofit Organizations: Profitable Careers with Nonprofits.* Manassas Park, VA: Impact Publications, 1998.

- Lauber, Daniel. *Nonprofit and Education Job Finder: 1997–2000.* River Forest, IL: Planning/ Communications, 1997.

Selected Nonprofit Reading

- Hodgkinson, Virginia Ann, Murray S. Weitzman, John A. Abrahams, Eric A. Crutchfield, and David R. Stevenson. *The Nonprofit Almanac 1996–1997: Dimensions of the Independent Sector.* San Francisco: Jossey-Bass Publishers, 1996.

- Letts, Christine W., William P. Ryan, and Allen S. Grossman. *High Performance Nonprofit Organizations: Managing Upstream for Greater Impact.* New York: John Wiley & Sons, 1999.

- Oster, Sharon M. *Strategic Management for Nonprofit Organizations.* Oxford: Oxford University Press, 1995.

- Sagawa, Shirley, and Eli Segal. *Common Interest, Common Good: Creating Value through Business and Social Sector Partnerships.* Boston, MA: Harvard Business School Publishing, 1999.

- Salamon, Lester. *America's Nonprofit Sector: A Primer.* New York: The Foundation Center, 1992.

- Salamon, Lester. *Holding the Center: America's Nonprofit Sector at a Crossroads.* New York: The Foundation Center, 1997. Available from the Nathan

Cummings Foundation, (212) 787-7300 or
<www.ncf.org>.

- Salamon, Lester M., and Helmut K. Anheier. *The Emerging Nonprofit Sector: An Overview.* Manchester: Manchester University Press, 1996.

- Shore, Bill, and Gloria Naylor. *Revolution of the Heart: A New Strategy for Creating Wealth and Meaningful Change.* New York: Riverhead Books, 1996.

Volunteering and Board Membership Resources

Volunteering

National "Volunteer Brokers"

- Americorps, <www.americorps.org> or (800) 220-6316

- "CityCares" organizations (e.g., Boston Cares, NYCares), <www.citycares.org>

- Points of Light Foundation (focuses on corporate volunteer opportunities), <www.pointsoflight.org> or (202) 729-8000

- United Way Voluntary Action Center (Boston), <www.uwmb.org> or (617) 624-8186

- Volunteer–The National Center, (703) 276-0542

- Volunteers of America, <www.voa.org> or (800) 899-0089

Publications

- Carroll, Andrew, and Christopher Miller. *Volunteer USA.* New York: Ballantine Books, 1991. (800) 733-3000.

- O'Connell, Brian, and Rebecca Buffum Taylor. *Voices from the Heart: In Celebration of America's Volunteers.* San Francisco: Jossey-Bass, 1998. (800) 956-7739

Board Membership

Organizations

- National Center for Nonprofit Boards, (800) 883-6262 or <www.ncnb.org>

- United Way BoardBank. Boston BoardBank, <www.uwmb.org> or (617) 624-8135

Publications

- Bowen, William G. "When a Business Leader Joins a Nonprofit Board." *Harvard Business Review* (September–October 1994): 38–43.

- Carver, John, and Alan Shrader, eds. *Boards That Make a Difference: A New Design for Leadership in Nonprofit and Public Organizations.* San Francisco: Jossey-Bass, 1997.

- Herzlinger, Regina E. "Effective Oversight: A Guide for Nonprofit Directors." *Harvard Business Review* (July–August 1994): 52–60.

- Ingram, Richard T. *Ten Basic Responsibilities of Nonprofit Boards.* Washington D.C.: National Center for Nonprofit Boards, 1996.

- Stoesz, Edgar and Chester Raber. *Doing Good Better! How to Be an Effective Board Member of a Nonprofit Organization.* Intercourse, PA: Good Books, 1997. Available through <www.opengroup.com/books>

- Taylor, Barbara E., Richard P. Chait, and Thomas P. Holland. "New Work of the Nonprofit Board." *Harvard Business Review* (September–October 1996): 36–46.

Arts and Culture Resources

Associations

- American Association of Museums, <www.aam-us.org>

- The American Symphony Orchestra League, <www.symphony.org>

- Dance/USA, <www.artswire.org/artswire/danceusa>

- International Society for the Performing Arts, <www.ispa-online.org>

- Opera America, <www.operaam.org>

- Symphony Orchestra Institute, <www.soi.org>

Publications

- Kotler, Philip, and Joanne Scheff. *Standing Room Only: Strategies for Marketing the Performing Arts.* Boston, MA: Harvard Business School Press, 1996.

- Langley, Stephen, and James Abruzzo. *Jobs in Arts and Media Management, 1992–1993.* New York: American Council for the Arts, 1992.

- Scheff, Joanne, and Philip Kotler. "How the Arts Can Prosper Through Strategic Collaborations." *Harvard Business Review* (January–February 1996): 52–62.

Harvard Business School Cases

- Hackman, J. Richard, Erin Lehman, and Adam Galinsky. "London Symphony Orchestra." Case 9-494-034. 1994.

- Hart, Christopher W. L., Jaime I. Ayala, and Julie K. Falstad. "American Repertory Theater–1988." Case 9-688-120. 1988.

- Poorvu, William J. "Isabella Stewart Gardner Museum." Case 9-395-137. 1994.

- Salter, Malcolm S. "Boston Symphony Orchestra." Case 9-375-340. 1983.

Organizations

Arts/Boston
100 Boylston Street
Suite 735
Boston, MA 02116
(617) 423-1345
<www.boston.com/artsboston>

Boston Ballet
19 Clarendon Street
Boston, MA 02116
(617) 695-6950
<www.boston.com/bostonballet>

Boston Children's Museum
300 Congress Street
Boston, MA 02210
(617) 426-6500

Boston Symphony Orchestra
Symphony Hall
Boston, MA 02115
(617) 266-1492
<www.bso.org>

Children's Television Workshop
One Lincoln Plaza
New York, NY 10023
(212) 595-3456
<www.ctw.org>

The Field Museum of Natural History
Roosevelt Road at Lake Shore Drive
Chicago, IL 60605
(312) 922-9410
<www.fmnh.org>

Guggenheim Museum
1071 Fifth Avenue
New York, NY 10128
(212) 423-3500
<www.guggenheim.org/srgm>

Isabella Stewart Gardner Museum
2 Palace Road
Boston, MA 02115
(617) 566-1401
<www.boston.com/gardner>

Lincoln Center for the Performing Arts
70 Lincoln Center Plaza
New York, NY 10023-6583

Metropolitan Museum of Art
1000 Fifth Avenue
New York, NY 10028
(212) 535-7710
<www.metmuseum.org>

Monterey Bay Aquarium
886 Cannery Road
Monterey, CA 93940
(408) 648-7902
<www.mbayaq.org>

Museum of Contemporary Art
237 East Ontario
Chicago, IL 60611
(312) 397-4050
<www.mcachicago.org>

Museum of Fine Arts, Boston
465 Huntington Ave
Boston, MA 02115
(617) 267-9300
<www.mfa.org>

Museum of Science, Boston
Science Park
Boston, MA 02114-1099
(617) 589-0123
<www.mos.org>

Museum of Television and Radio
25 West 52nd Street
New York, NY 10019
(212) 621-6600
<www.mtr.org>

Mystic Seaport Museum
PO Box 6000
Mystic, CT 06335
(860) 572-0711
<www.mysticseaport.org>

New England Aquarium
177 Milk Street
Boston, MA 02110
(617) 973-0289
<www.neaq.org>

New England Conservatory of Music
290 Huntington Avenue
Boston, MA 02215
(617) 262-1120

Philadelphia Museum of Art
Benjamin Franklin Parkway
Box 7646
Philadelphia, PA 19101
(215) 541-7800
<http://pma.libertynet.org>

San Diego Zoo
PO Box 551
San Diego, CA 92112
(619) 557-3968
<www.sandiegozoo.org>

Whitney Museum of Art
945 Madison Avenue
New York, NY 10021
(212) 570-3645
<www.echonyc.com/~whitney>

WGBH Educational Foundation
125 Western Avenue
Boston, MA 02134
(617) 492-2777
<www.boston.com/wgbh>

Community Economic Development Resources

Associations

- Local Initiative Support Corporation (LISC), (212) 455-9900

- National Community Building Network, (510) 893-2404

- U.S. Department of Housing and Urban Development (HUD), Washington D.C., <www.hud.gov>

Publications

- Ards, Angela. *Community Pride: Reclaiming a Neighborhood in Central Harlem.* Available from the Edna McConnell Clark Foundation, (212) 551-9100.

- DeParle, Jason. "Shrinking Welfare Rolls Leave Record High Share of Minorities." *New York Times,* 27 July 1998.

- Porter, Michael E. "The Competitive Advantage of the Inner City." *Harvard Business Review* (May–June 1995): 55–71.

- Schorr, Lisbeth B. *Common Purpose: Strengthening Families and Neighborhoods to Rebuild America.* New York: Doubleday, 1997.

Harvard Business School Cases

- Austin, James E., and Andrea L. Strimling. "Cleveland Turnaround (A): Responding to the Crisis—1978–88." Case 9-796-151. 1996.

- Austin, James E., and Andrea L. Strimling. "Cleveland Turnaround (B): Building on Progress—1989–96." Case 9-796-152. 1996.

- Austin, James E., and Andrea L. Strimling. "Cleveland Turnaround (C): Facts and Figures." Case 9-796-153. 1996.

- Austin, James E., and Andrea L. Strimling. "Cleveland Turnaround (D): Challenges for the Future." Case 9-796-154. 1996.

- Burakoff, Robert. "STRIVE." Case 9-399-054. 1998.

- Heskett, James L., and Roger Hallowell. "Bidwell Training Center, Inc. and Manchester Craftsmen's Guild: Preparation in Pittsburgh." Case 9-693-087. 1993.

- Poorvu, William J., and John H. Vogel Jr. "Forest-Glen Cooperative." Case 9-395-057. 1994.

Organizations

Action for Boston Community Development
178 Tremont Street
Boston, MA 02111
(617) 357-6000
<www.bostonabcd.org>

Bidwell Training Center Inc./Manchester Craftsman's Guild
1815 Metropolitan Street
Pittsburgh, PA 15233
(412) 322-1773

Coastal Enterprises Inc.
PO Box 268
Water Street
Wiscasset, ME 04578
(207) 882-7552

Common Ground/Times Square Job Training Corporation
255 W 43rd Street
New York, NY 10036
(212) 768-8989

The Community Builders Inc.
95 Berkeley Street
Boston, MA 02116
(617) 695-9595
<www.tcbinc.org>

East Harlem Employment Service Inc./STRIVE
1820 Lexington Avenue
New York, NY 10029
(212) 360-1100
<www.strive-ehes.org>

The Enterprise Foundation
10227 Wincopin Circle
Suite 500
Columbia, MD 21044
(410) 964-1230

Habitat for Humanity
121 Habitat Street
Americus, GA 31709
1-800-HABITAT
<www.habitat.org>

The ICA Group
20 Park Plaza
Suite 1127
Boston, MA 02116
(617) 338-0010

Initiative for a Competitive Inner City
727 Atlantic Avenue
Suite 600
Boston, MA 02111
(617) 292-2363

Jobs for the Future
One Bowdoin Square
Boston, MA 02114
(617) 742-5995

LISC
733 Third Avenue
Room 8
New York, NY 10017
(212) 455-9900

National Community Reinvestment Coalition
1875 Connecticut Avenue, NW
Suite 1010
Washington, DC 20009
(202) 986-7898

New Community Corporation
233 West Market Street
Newark, NJ 07103
(201) 623-2800

Osage Initiatives
111 Osage Street
Denver, CO 80204
(303) 892-8300

Phipps House
43 West 23rd Street
Eighth Floor
New York, NY
(212) 243-9090

Upper Manhattan Empowerment Zone
290 Lenox Avenue
New York, NY 10027
(212) 410-0030

Community Development Financial Institutions Resources

Associations

- CDFI Coalition, <www.cdfi.org> or (215) 923-5363

- National Community Capital Association, <www.communitycapital.org> or (215) 923-4754

- National Federation of Community Development Credit Unions, <www.natfed.org>

Harvard Business School Cases

- Austin, James E., "Women's World Banking." Case 9-391-163. 1991.

- Austin, James E., and Enrique Ogliastri. "Corposol." Case 9-796-142. 1996.

- Dees, J. Gregory, and Christine C. Remey. "BayBank Boston." Case 9-393-095. 1993.

- Dees, J. Gregory, and Christine C. Remey. "Shorebank Corporation." Case 9-393-096. 1993.

- Kanter, Rosabeth Moss. "First Community Bank." Case 9-396-202. 1996.

- Lerner, Joshua, and Erik K. Jackson. "Northeast Ventures: January 1996." Case 9-296-093. 1996.

Organizations

Boston Community Capital
30 Germania Street
Boston, MA 02130
(617) 522-6768

Center for Women & Enterprise
45 Bromfield Street
Sixth Floor
Boston, MA 02108
(617) 423-3001

Community Economic Development Assistance Corporation (CEDAC)
18 Tremont Street
Suite 1020
Boston, MA 02108
(617) 727-5944

Corporation for Enterprise Development
National Office
777 North Capitol Street, NE
Suite 410
Washington, DC 20002
(202) 408-9788

The Development Fund
231 Sansome Street
Sixth Floor
San Francisco, CA 94104

First Community Bank
c/o BankBoston
100 Federal Street
PO Box 2016
Boston, MA 02110

New York City Investment Fund
One Battery Park Plaza
New York, NY 10004
(212) 493-7551

Roberts Enterprise Development Fund
Presidio Building 1009
First Floor
PO Box 29266
San Francisco, CA 94129
(415) 561-6677
<www.redf.org>

Self-Help Ventures Fund
301 West Main Street
Durham, NC 27701
(800) 476-7428
<www.self-help.org>

Shorebank
7054 South Jeffery Boulevard
Chicago, IL 60649
(773) 753-5702

Women's World Banking
8 West 40th Street
New York, NY 10018
(212) 768-8515

Education Resources

Associations

- The Education Industry Group, <www.eindustry.com>

- The Harvard Project on Schooling and Children, (617) 496-4938

- The National Association for Independent Schools, (202) 973-9700

- The National Parent Teacher Association, <www.pta.com>

- The National School Board Association, <www.nsba.org>

Publications

- *The Chronicle of Higher Education,* weekly. <http://chronicle.com>

- *The Education Industry Report.* Education Industry Group, monthly. (888) 864-3834.

- *Education Week,* <www.edweek.org>

- *The Elementary School Journal.* University of Chicago Press. Five issues per year.

- Kidder, Tracy. *Among Schoolchildren.* New York: Avon Books, 1990.

- Steinberg, Laurence, B., Bradford Brown, and Sanford M. Dornbusch. *Beyond the Classroom: Why School Reform Has Failed and What Parents Need to Do.* New York: Touchstone, 1999.

Harvard Business School Cases

- Dees, J. Gregory, and Jaan Elias. "Education Alternatives, Inc." Case 9-395-106. 1994.

- Dees, J. Gregory, and James T. Sparkman. "Nobel Education Dynamics, Inc." Case 9-396-281. 1996.

- Dees, J. Gregory, and Susan S. Harmeling. "Education for Profit: Edison and EAI." Case 9-393-114. 1993.

- Gabarro, John J. "Thurgood Marshall High School." Case 9-494-070. 1993.

- Lovelock, Christopher H. "Hood College (Condensed)." Case 9-579-500. 1978.

- Rangan, V. Kasturi, Katherine K. Merseth, and Marie Bell. "Charter Schools: Setting the Course?" Case 9-597-059. 1996.

Organizations

Bright Horizons
One Kendall Square
Building 200
Cambridge, MA 02139
617-577-8020
<www.brighthorizons.com>

The Edison Project
521 Fifth Avenue
15th Floor
New York, NY 10175
(212) 419-1600
<www.edisonproject.com>

Educational Alternatives
7900 Xerxes Avenue
Suite 1300
Bloomington, MN 55431
(612) 832-0092

EF Education
EF Center Boston
One Education Street
Cambridge, MA 02141
(617) 619-1028
<www.ef.com>

Harvard Business School Executive Education
Harvard Business School
Glass Hall
Boston, MA 02163
(617) 495-6789

Head Start National Association
Mary E. Switzer Building
330 C Street, SW
Room 2050
Washington, DC 20013

Institute of International Education
809 United Nations Plaza
New York, NY 10016
(212) 883-8200

Junior Achievement
One Education Way
Colorado Springs, CO 80906
(719) 540-8000
<www.ja.org>

Kaplan Educational Centers
888 Seventh Avenue
New York, NY 10106
<www.kaplan.com>

The Learning Company
One Athenaeum Street
Cambridge, MA 02142
(617) 494-1200
<www.learningco.com>

The Learning Contract
2477 Vallejo Street
San Francisco, CA 94123
<www.projectachieve.com>

NFTE (National Foundation for Teaching Entrepreneurship)
120 Wall Street
29th Floor
New York, NY 10005
(212) 978-0112

Outward Bound
Route 9D, R2 Box 280
Garrison, NY 10524-9757
(800) 243-8520
<www.outwardbound.org>

Reading Is Fundamental
600 Maryland Avenue, SW
Suite 600
Washington, DC 20024
(202) 287-3220
<www.rif.org>

Shackleton Schools
36 Bromfield Street
Suite 500
Boston, MA 02108
(617) 357-5100
<www.shackleton.org>

Sylvan Learning Centers
1000 Lancaster Street
Baltimore, MD 21202
(410) 843-8000
<www.educate.com>

Teach for America
20 Exchange Place
8th Floor
New York, NY 10005
(212) 425-9039

Environment Resources

Associations

- Environmental Careers Organization, (617) 426-4375

- Environmental Career Opportunities, <http://ecojobs.com/>

- Environmental Careers World, <http://environmental-jobs.com>

Publications

- Biddle, David. "Recycling for Profit: The New Green Business Frontier." *Harvard Business Review* (November–December 1993): 145–156.

- Environmental Careers Organization and Bill Sharp. *The New Complete Guide to Environmental Careers.* Washington, D.C.: Island Press, 1993. <www.islandpress.org> or (800) 828-1302.

- Porter, Michael E., and Claas van der Linde. "Green and Competitive: Ending the Stalemate." *Harvard Business Review* (September–October 1995): 120–134.

- Sawhill, John, Alice Howard, and Joan Magretta. "Surviving Success: An Interview with the Nature Conservancy's John Sawhill." *Harvard Business Review* (September–October 1995): 108–118.

- Walley, Noah, and Bradley Whitehead. "It's Not Easy Being Green." *Harvard Business Review* (May–June, 1994): 46–52.

Harvard Business School Cases

- Livesey, Sharon M. "McDonalds and the Environment." Case 9-391-108. 1990.

- Reinhardt, Forest, and Thomas A. Patterson. "Montana Land Reliance." Case 9-794-050. 1993.

Organizations

Appalachian Mountain Club
5 Joy Street
Boston, MA 02108
(617) 523-0636
<www.outdoors.org>

Arnold Arboretum
125 Arborway
Jamaica Plain, MA 02130
(617) 524-1718
<www.arboretum.harvard.edu>

Chesapeake Bay Foundation
162 Prince George Street
Annapolis, MD 21401
(301) 627-4393

Coalition for Environmentally Responsible Economies (CERES)
11 Arlington Street
Sixth Floor
Boston, MA 02116
(617) 247-0700
<www.ceres.org>

Earthwatch
PO Box 403
680 Mt. Auburn Street
Watertown, MA 02272
(617) 926-8200

Environmental Action Foundation
6930 Carroll Avenue
Suite 600
Takoma Park, MD 20912
(301) 891-1100

Environmental Defense Fund
1875 Connecticut Avenue, NW
Washington, DC 20009
(202) 387-3500
<www.edf.org>

Greenpeace
1436 U Street, NW
Washington, DC 20009
(202) 462-4507

National Audubon Society
(ask about local chapters)
700 Broadway
New York, NY 10003
(212) 979-3000
<www.audubon.org/>

National Wildlife Federation
8925 Leesburg Pike
Vienna, VA 22184
(703) 790-4522
<www.nwf.org/nwf>

The Nature Conservancy
1815 North Lynn Street
Arlington, VA 22209
(703) 247-3721 (job hotline)
<www.tnc.org>

Rails to Trails Conservancy
1100 17th Street, NW
10th Floor
Washington, DC 20036
(202) 331-9696
<www.railtrails.org/>

Rainforest Action Network
221 Pine Street
Suite 500
San Francisco, CA 94104
(415) 398-4404
<www.ran.org/ran>

The Sierra Club
85 Second Street
Second Floor
San Francisco, CA 94105
(415) 977-5500
<www.sierraclub.org>

Trust for Public Land
116 New Montgomery
Fourth Floor
San Francisco, CA 94105
(415) 495-4014
<www.igc.org/tpl/>

The Wilderness Society
900 17th Street, NW
Washington, DC 20006
(202) 833-2300
<www.wilderness.org>

World Resources Institute (WRI)
1709 New York Avenue, NW
Washington, DC 20006
(202) 638-6300
<www.wri.org>

World Wildlife Fund
1250 24th Street, NW
Washington, DC 20037
(202) 293-4800

Foundations Resources

Associations

- Associated Grantmakers of Massachusetts, (617-426-2606)

- Council on Foundations, <www.cof.org>

- The Foundation Center, <www.fdncenter.org>

- National Network of Grantmakers, (619) 220-0690

Publications

- The Foundation Center. *The Foundation Directory.* 21st ed. New York: The Foundation Center, 1999.

- *Foundation News and Commentary.* Washington, D.C.: Council on Foundations, <www.cof.org>

- Freeman, David F. *The Handbook on Private Foundations.* New York: The Foundation Center, 1991.

- Letts, Christine W., William Ryan, and Allen Grossman. "Virtuous Capital: What Foundations Can Learn from Venture Capitalists." *Harvard Business Review* (March–April 1997): 36–44.

Harvard Business School Cases

- Austin, James E., and Linda Carrigan. "The Harbus Foundation." Case 9-399-031. 1998.

Organizations

Andrew Mellon Foundation
140 East 62nd Street
New York, NY 10021
(212) 838-8400
<www.mellon.org>

Annie E. Casey Foundation
701 St. Paul Street
Baltimore, MD 21202
(410) 547-6600
<www.aecf.org>

The Boston Foundation
One Boston Place
24th Floor
Boston, MA 02108-4402
(617) 723-7415
<www.tbf.org>

Cleveland Foundation
1422 Euclid Avenue
Suite 1400
Cleveland, OH 44115
(216) 861-3810

David and Lucille Packard Foundation
300 Second Street
Suite 200
Los Altos, CA 94022
(415) 948-7658
<www.packfound.org>

DeWitt Wallace-Readers Digest Fund
Two Park Avenue
23rd Floor
New York, NY 10016
(212) 251-9800
<www.wallacefunds.org>

Edna McConnell Clark Foundation
250 Park Avenue
Suite 900
New York, NY 10177

Ewing Marion Kauffman Foundation
4900 Oak Street
Kansas City, MO 64112
(816)-932-1000
<www.emkf.org>

Ford Foundation
320 East 43rd Street
New York, NY 10017
(212) 573-5000
<www.fordfound.org>

Getty Trust
1200 Getty Center Drive
Suite 800
Los Angeles, CA 90049
(310) 440-7320

The Heinz Endowments
30 CNG Tower
625 Liberty Ave
Pittsburgh, PA 15222
<www.heinz.org>

John D. and Catherine T. MacArthur Foundation
140 South Dearborn Street
Suite 1100
Chicago, IL 60603
(312) 726-8000
<www.macfdn.org>

The Kellogg Foundation
One Michigan Avenue East
Battle Creek, MI 49017
(616) 968-1611
<www.wkkf.org>

New York Community Trust
Two Park Avenue
New York, NY 10016
(212) 686-0010

The Pew Charitable Trusts
2005 Market Street
Suite 1700
Philadelphia, PA 19103
(215) 575-9050
<www.pewtrusts.com>

Robert Wood Johnson Foundation
PO Box 2316
Princeton, NJ 08543
(609) 452-8701
<www.rwjf.org>

Rockefeller Foundation
420 Fifth Avenue
New York, NY 10018-2702
(212) 869-8500
<www.rockfound.org>

Soros Foundations Network
400 West 59th Street
New York, NY 10019
<www.soros.org>

Surdna Foundation
330 Madison Avenue
30th Floor
New York, NY 10017-5001
(212) 557-0010
<www.surdna.org/surdna>

Warren Weaver Fellows Program
c/o The Rockefeller Foundation
420 Fifth Avenue
New York, NY 10018
(212) 852-8407

Government Resources

Publications

- Carroll Publishing Company. *Carroll's Municipal/County Directory.* Washington, D.C.: Carroll Publishing Company, semiannual.

- Carroll Publishing Company. *Carroll's State Directory.* Washington, D.C.: Carroll Publishing Company, issued three times a year.

- Krannich, Ronald L., and Caryl Rae Krannich. *The Complete Guide to Public Employment.* 3rd ed. Manassas, VA: Impact Publications, 1994.

- Krannich, Ronald L., and Caryl Rae Krannich. *Find a Federal Job Fast: How to Cut the Red Tape and Get Hired.* 4th ed. Manassas, VA: Impact Publications, 1999.

- Monitor Leadership Publications. *The Federal Yellow Book.* Washington, D.C.: Monitor Leadership Directories, Inc., annual.

- Monitor Leadership Directories. *State Yellow Book: A Directory of the Executive, Legislative, and Judicial Branches of State Governments.* Washington, D.C.: Monitor Leadership Directories, Inc., annual.

- Ruffin, Albert, ed. *Carroll's Federal Directory 1997: Executive, Legislative, Judicial.* Washington, D.C.: Caroll Publishing Company, annual.

- Wehnes, Lynn Bracken. *The Harvard College Guide to Careers in Government and Politics.* Cambridge: Harvard University, Office of Career Services, 1992.

Harvard Business School Cases

- Goldsmith, Stephen. "Can Business Really Do Business with Government?" *Harvard Business Review* (May–June 1997): 110–121.

- Herzlinger, Regina E. "Can Public Trust in Nonprofits and Governments Be Restored?" *Harvard Business Review* (March–April 1996): 97–107.

- Mintzberg, Henry. "Managing Government, Governing Management." *Harvard Business Review* (May–June 1996): 75–83.

- Osborne, David, Bruce G. Posner, and Lawrence R. Rothstein. "Reinventing the Business of Government: An Interview with Change Catalyst David Osborne." *Harvard Business Review* (May–June 1994): 132–143.

Organizations

Congressional Budget Office
Ford House Office Building
Second and D Streets, SW
Room 430
Washington, DC 20515
(202) 226-2800
<www.cbo.gov>

The Foreign Service
<www.state.gov/www/careers>

Presidential Management Internship Program (PMI)
<www.usajobs.opm.gov>

U.S. Department of State
Recruitment Division/Exam
PO Box 12226
Arlington, VA 22219

White House Fellows Program
(202) 395-4522 or <www.whitehouse.gov/WH_Fellows>

World Bank
Young Professionals Program
1818 H Street, NW
Room 55-068
Washington, DC 20433

Health Care Resources

Associations

- American Hospital Association, <www.aha.org>

- American Medical Association, <www.ama-assn.org>

- American Medical Group Association, <www.amga.org>

Publications

- Donelan, Karen, Robert J. Blendon, George D. Lundberg, David B. Calkins, Joseph P. Newhouse, Lucian L. Leape, Dahlie K. Remler, and Humphrey Taylor. "The New Medical Marketplace: Physician's Views." *Health Affairs* 16, no. 5 (1998): 139–148.

- *Journal of the American Medical Association* (JAMA), <www.ama-assn.org/public/journals/jama>, weekly.

- Klass, Perri. "Managing Managed Care." *New York Times Magazine,* 5 October 1997, 72–76

Harvard Business School Cases

- Bohmer, Richard. "Note on Managed Care." Case 9-698-060. 1998.

- Dees, J. Gregory, Marc Boatwright, and Jaan Elias. "GuateSalud." Case 9-395-125. 1995.

- Dhebar, Anirudh. "Lincoln Community Hospital." Case 9-191-149. 1991.

- Friedman, Raymond A., and Caitlin Deinard. "Prepare/21 at Beth Israel Hospital (A)." Case 9-491-045. 1991.

- Herzlinger, Regina E. "Hyatt Hill Health Center." Case 9-190-009. 1989.

- Herzlinger, Regina E., and Ann Winslow. "The Financing of the U.S. Health Care System." Case Note 9-196-095. 1995.

- Herzlinger, Regina E., and Ramona K. Hilgenkap. "Empire Blue Cross and Blue Shield (A) (B) (C) (D) (E) (F) (G) (H)." Cases: 9-195-216; 9-195-217; 9-195-218; 9-195-219; 9-195-220; 9-195-221; 9-195-222; 9-195-223. 1995.

- Herzlinger, Regina E., and Wayne W. Adams. "South Eye Insitute." Case 9-193-140. 1993.

- McFarlan, F. Warren, and Jaan Elias. "Mt. Auburn Hospital." Case 9-397-083. 1996.

- Menezes, Melvyn A. J. "LifeSpan Inc.: Abbott Northwestern Hospital." Case 9-587-104. 1986.

- Rangan, V. Kasturi, and Sohel Karim. "New York Against AIDS (A): The Saatchi & Saatchi Compton Advertising Campaign." Case 9-590-036. 1990.

- Teisberg, Elizabeth O., and Eric J. Vayle. "Brigham and Women's Hospital in 1992." Case 9-792-095. 1992.

Organizations

American Cancer Society
1599 Clifton Road, N.E.
Atlanta, GA 30329
(800) 227-2345
<www.cancer.org>

American Diabetes Association
1660 Duke Street
Alexandria, VA 22314
<www.diabetes.org>

American Heart Association
7272 Greenville Avenue
Dallas, TX 75231-4596
(214) 706-1341
<www.amhrt.org>

American Lung Association
1740 Broadway
New York, NY 10019-4374
(212) 315-8700
<www.lungusa.org>

Brigham and Women's Hospital
75 Francis Street
Boston, MA 02115
(617) 732-5500

Cedars-Sinai Medical Center
8723 Alden Drive, ASB1
Los Angeles, CA 90048
(310) 855-5521

Cleveland Clinic Foundation
9500 Euclid Avenue
Cleveland, OH 44195
(216) 444-2705
<www.ccf.org>

Dana-Farber Cancer Institute
44 Binney Street
Boston, MA 02115
(617) 632-3052
<www.jimmyfund.com>

March of Dimes
1275 Mamaroneck Avenue
White Plains, NY 10605
(914) 428-7100
<www.modimes.org>

**Massachusetts General Hospital Corporation/
Partners HealthCare**
55 Fruit Street
Boston, MA 02114
(617) 724-2266
<www.mgh.harvard.edu>

New York Hospital
525 East 68th Street
New York, NY 10021
(212) 746-5454

Planned Parenthood Federation of America, Inc.
810 Seventh Avenue
New York, NY 10019
(212) 541-7800
<www.ppfa.org/ppfa/>

International Aid and Economic Development Resources

Associations

- InterAction, <www.interaction.org>

- International Affairs Web Directory, <www.eff.org/govt>

- International Jobs, <www.state.gov/www/issues/unvacant>

- U.S. Agency for International Development, <www.info.usaid.gov>

Harvard Business School Cases

- Austin, James E. "Oxfam America." Case 9-798-036. 1997.

- Austin, James E. "Women's World Banking." Case 9-391-163. 1991.

- Austin, James E., and Enrique Ogliastri. "Corposol." Case 9-796-142. 1997.

- Dees, J. Gregory, Robert Larson, and Jaan Elias. "BRAC (Bangladesh Rural Advancement Committee." Case 9-395-107. 1995.

- Donnellon, Anne, James Reed, and Nicholas Richardson. "In the Shadow of the City." Case 9-490-093. 1990.

- Kennedy, Robert E., and Katherine Marquis. "China: Facing the 21st Century." Case 9-798-066. 1998.

- Lodge, George C. "World Bank: Mission Uncertain." Case 9-792-100. 1992.

- Pill, Huw, and Courtenay Sprague. "Uganda and the Washington Consensus." Case 9-798-047. 1998.

- Rangan, V. Kasturi. "Population Services International: The Social Marketing Project in Bangladesh." Case 9-586-013. 1985.

- Reinhardt, Forest, and Kimberly O'Neill Packard. "Global Climate Change." Case 9-798-076. 1998.

- Vietor, Richard H. K., and Edward Prewitt. "Reconstruction of Zambia." Case 9-792-089. 1992.

- Wells Jr., Louis T. "Enron Development Corp.: The Dabhol Power Project in Maharashtra India." Case 9-797-085. 1997.

Organizations

ACCION International
120 Beacon Street
Somerville, MA 02143
(617) 492-4930
<www.accion.org>

American Red Cross
8111 Gatehouse Road
Third Floor
Falls Church, VA 22042
(702) 206-6006
<www.redcross.org>

Americares
161 Cherry Street
New Canaan, CT 06840
800-486-HELP
<www.americares.org>

Amnesty International
322 Eighth Avenue
10th Floor
New York, NY 10001
(212) 807-8400
<www.amnesty.org>

CARE
151 Ellis Street
Atlanta, GA 30303
(404) 681-2552
<www.care.org>

Catholic Relief Services
209 West Fayette Street
Baltimore, MD 21201
800-235-2772
<www.devcap.org/crs>

European Bank for Reconstruction and Development (EBRD)
One Exchange Square
London EC2A 2JN
United Kingdom
44 171 338 6000

Inter-American Development Bank
E0517/APDBS
1300 New York Avenue, NW
Washington, DC 20577
(202) 623-1000
<www.iadb.org>

The International Finance Corporation
Recruitment Division
Room 11K-292
2121 Pennsylvania Avenue, NW
Washington, DC 20433
<www.ifc.org>

International Monetary Fund
Recruitment Division
IS9-100
Washington, DC 20431
<www.imf.org>

International Rescue Committee
122 East 42nd Street
New York, NY 10168
(212) 551-3000
<www.intrescom.org>

Organisation for Economic Co-Operation and Development (OECD)
2 rue André-Pascal,
75775 Paris CEDEX 16
France
<www.oecd.org>

Oxfam America
26 West Street
Boston, MA 02111
800-77-OXFAM
<www.oxfamamerica.org>

Population Services International
1120 19th Street, NW
Washington, DC 20036
<www.psiwash.org>

Save the Children
54 Wilton Road
Westport, CT 06880
(203) 221-4000

UNICEF
333 East 38th Street
Suite 1112
New York, NY 10016
(212) 686-5522
<www.unicef.org>

United Nations
Office of Human Resources Management
Room S-2555
New York, NY 10017

United Nations Internship Programme
Room S-2580
Office of Human Resources Management
New York, NY 10017
<www.un.org>

Women's World Banking (WWB)
8 West 40th Street
New York, NY 10018
(212) 768-8515

World Trade Organization
Personnel Division
154 Rue de Lausanne
Geneva
Switzerland 1211 CH-21
<www.wto.org>

World Vision
919 West Huntington Drive
Monrovia, CA 91016
(818) 357-7979

Social Services Resources

Associations

- Children, Youth and Family Consortium's Electronic Clearinghouse, <www.cyfc.umn.edu>

- National Alliance to End Homelessness, <www.naeh.org>

- National Association of Child Care Professionals, <www.naccp.org>

- National Center on Addiction and Substance Abuse at Columbia University, <www.casacolumbia.org>

- National Coalition for the Homeless, <nch.ari.net>

- National Council on Aging (NCOA), <www.ncoa.org>

- Welfare Information Network, <www.welfareinfo.org/bestprac.htm>

Publications

- Carnegie Foundation. *Starting Points: Meeting the Needs of Our Youngest Children.* New York: The Carnegie Foundation, 1994. <www.carnegie.org/starting_points>

- The Packard Foundation. *The Future of Children.* (published four times annually). Available at <www.futureofchildren.org>

- Substance Abuse and Mental Health Services Administration. *National Directory of Drug Abuse and Alcoholism Treatment and Prevention Programs.* Washington, D.C.: Government Printing Office. <www.health.org/search/treatdir96.htm>

Harvard Business School Cases

- Bell, David E., and Ann Leamon. "The United Way of Massachusetts Bay." Case 9-599-042. 1998.

- Bradach, Jeffrey L., and Nicole Sackley. "City Year Expansion: National Strategy (A)." Case 9-496-001. 1995.

- Greyser, Stephen A. "Greater Gotham United Way." Case 9-594-004. 1993.

- Loveman, Gary, and Andrew Slavitt. "Habitat for Humanity International." Case 9-694-038. 1993.

- Shapiro, Benson P., and Robert N. Clarke. "Richardson Center for the Blind." Case 9-573-004. 1972.

Organizations

Adoptive Families of America
2309 Como Avenue
St Paul, MN 55108
800-372-3300
<www.adoptivefam.org>

Alcoholics Anonymous
470 Riverside Drive
New York, NY 10163
(212) 870-3400
<www.aa.org>

Battered Women's Alternatives
PO Box 6406
Concord, CA 94524
(925) 676-2845

Big Brothers/Big Sisters of America
230 North 13th Street
Philadelphia, PA 19107
(215) 567-7000
<www.bbbsa.org>

Boys and Girls Clubs of America
1230 West Peachtree Street, NW
Atlanta, GA 30309
(404) 815-5700
<www.bgca.org>

Boy Scouts of America
1325 West Walnut Hill Lane
PO Box 152079
Irving, TX 75015-2079
(972) 580-2000
<www.bsa.scouting.org>

Center for Employment and Training
701 Vine Street
San Jose, CA 95110
(408) 287-7924

The Children's Aid Society
105 East 22nd Street
New York, NY 10010
(212) 358-8930

Children's Defense Fund
25 E Street, NW
Washington, DC 20001
(202) 628-8787
<www.childrensdefense.org>

City Year
285 Columbus Avenue
Boston, MA 02116
(617) 927-2500
<ww.city-year.org>

Common Cause
1250 Connecticut Avenue, NW
Washington, DC 20036

Food for the Hungry
7729 East Greenway Road
Scottsdale, AZ 85260
(800) 248-6437
<www.fh.org>

Girl Scouts of the USA
420 Fifth Avenue
New York, NY 10018-2702
(212) 852-8000
<www.girlscouts.org>

Goodwill Industries
9200 Rockville Pike
Bethesda, MD 20814
(310) 530-6500
<www.goodwill.org>

Habitat For Humanity
121 Habitat Street
Americus, GA 31709
(912) 924-6935
<www.habitat.org>

Hazelden
CO 3, PO Box 11
Center City, MN, 55012
<www.hazelden.org>

Make-a-Wish Foundation
100 West Clarendon Avenue
Suite 2200
Phoenix, AZ 85013
(800) 722-WISH
<www.wish.org>

National Coalition for the Homeless
1012 14th Street, NW
Suite 600
Washington, DC 20005
(202) 737-6444
<http://nch.ari.net>

Pioneer Human Services
2200 Rainier Avenue South
Seattle, WA 98144
(206) 322-6645

Program for Young Negotiators
432 Columbia Street
Suite B6-7
Cambridge, MA 02141

Project Renewal
200 Varick Street
Ninth Floor
New York, NY 10010
(212) 620-0340

Public Allies
1015 18th Street, NW
Suite 200
Washington, DC 20036
(202) 822-1180
<www.publicallies.org>

The Salvation Army
615 Slaters Lane
Alexandria, VA 22313
(703) 684-5500
<www.salvationarmyusa.org>

Second Harvest
116 Michigan Avenue
Suite 4
Chicago, IL 60603
(312) 263-2303
<www.secondharvest.org>

Share Our Strength
1511 K. Street, NW
Suite 940
Washington, DC 20005
(202) 393-2925

Union Settlement Association
237 East 104th Street
New York, NY 10029
(212) 828-6000

United Neighborhood Houses of New York
70 West 36th Street
5th Floor
New York, NY 10018
(212) 967-0322
<www.unhny.org>

United Way of America
701 North Fairfax Street
Alexandria, VA 22314
<www.unitedway.org>

Victim's Services
2 Lafayette Street
New York, NY 10007
(212) 577-7700

YMCA
101 North Wacker Drive
Chicago, IL 60606
(312) 269-1185
<www.ymca.net>

YWCA
726 Broadway
New York, NY 10003
(212) 614-2700

Social Purpose Businesses Resources

Associations

- National Center for Social Entrepreneurs, <www.socialentrepreneurs.org> or (800) 696-4066

Publications

- Emerson, Jed. *New Social Entrepreneurs: The Success, Challenge and Lessons of Non-Profit Enterprise Creation*. Minneapolis: National Center for Social Entrepreneurs, 1998. Available from National Center for Social Entrepreneurs, <www. socialentrepreneurs.org>

- Shore, Bill, and Gloria Naylor. *Revolution of the Heart: A New Strategy for Creating Wealth and Meaningful Change*. New York: Riverhead Books, 1996.

- *Who Cares*. Washington, D.C.: Who Cares Inc., bimonthly. (800) 628-1692 or <www.whocares.org>

Harvard Business School Cases

- Austin, James. E., and Meredith D. Pearson. "Community Wealth Ventures, Inc." Case 9-399-023. 1998.

- Dees, J. Gregory. "Social Enterprise: Private Initiatives for the Common Good." Case 9-395-116. 1994.

- Dees, J. Gregory, and Alice Oberfield. "Rainforest Crunch." Case 9-391-132. 1991.

- Hardt, Myra, Marco Iansiti, Andrea Chermayeff, and Diana Gardner. "CitySoft, Inc." Case 9-698-080. 1998.

Organizations

Ashoka: Innovators for the Public
1700 North Moore Street
Suite 1920
Arlington, VA 22209
<www.ashoka.org>

Beansprout Networks
37 Broadway
Suite 3
Arlington, MA 02474
(781) 648-2826 ext. 11
<www.beansprout.com>

CitySoft
160 Second Street
Cambridge, MA 02142
(617) 354-8113
<www.citysoft.com>

Community Wealth Ventures
240 West 35th Street
Suite 505
New York, NY 10001
(212) 563-3077

The Conservation Company
1617 JFK Boulevard
Suite 1550
Philadelphia, PA 19103

Juma Ventures
116 New Montgomery Street
Suite 600
San Francisco, CA 94105
(415) 247-6580

NewProfit Inc.
285 Columbus Avenue
Fifth Floor
Boston, MA 02116
(617) 927-2510

Roberts Enterprise Development Fund
Presidio Building 1009
First Floor
PO Box 29266
San Francisco, CA 94129
(415) 561-6677
<www.redf.org>

SocialGoods
49 Rice Road
Wayland, MA 01778
(617) 783-8307

Worksource Staffing Partnership Inc.
20 Park Plaza
Suite 1126
Boston, MA 02116
(617) 423-7256

Socially Responsible Business/Corporate Community Relations Resources

Associations

• Boston College Center for Corporate Community Relations, <www.bc.edu/cccr> or (617) 552-4545

• Business for Social Responsibility (BSR), <www.bsr.org> or (202) 842-5400

• Net Impact (formerly Students for Responsible Business), <www.net-impact.org> or (415) 778-8366

Publications

• Albion, Mark S. *Making a Life, Making a Living: Reclaiming Your Purpose and Passion in Business and in Life.* New York: Warner Books, 2000.

• Makower, Joel. *Beyond the Bottom Line: Putting Social Responsibility to Work for Your Business and the World.* New York: Touchstone Books, 1995.

• Morgan, Hal, and Kerry Tucker. *Companies That Care.* New York: Simon and Schuster, 1991.

• Reder, Alan. *75 Best Business Practices for Socially Responsible Companies.* New York: G. P. Putnam's Sons, 1995.

• Weeden, Curt, Paul Newman, and Peter Lynch. *Corporate Social Investing: The Breakthrough Strategy for Giving and Getting Corporate Contributions.* San Francisco: Berrett-Koehler Publications, 1998.

Harvard Business School Cases

• Austin, James E. "Newman's Own, Inc." Case 9-399-052. 1998.

• Austin, James E., and Jaan Elias. "Timberland and Community Involvement." Case 9-796-156. 1996.

• Lodge, George C., and Jeffrey F. Rayport. "Responsible Care." Case 9-391-135. 1991.

• Piper, Thomas R., and Charles A. Nichols III. "The Poletown Dilemma." Case 9-389-017. 1988.

• Smith, Craig. "The New Corporate Philanthropy." *Harvard Business Review* (May–June 1994): 105–116.

Organizations

Ben & Jerry's
30 Community Drive
South Burlington, VT 05403-6828
(802) 651-9600
<www.benjerry.com>

Business for Social Responsibility
609 Mission Street
Second Floor
San Francisco, CA 94105
(415) 537-0888
<www.bsr.org>

Brody & Weiser
250 West Main Street
Suite 110
Brandford, CT 06405
(203) 481-4199
<www.brodyweiser.com>

Honest Tea
4905 DelRay Avenue
Bethesda, MD 20814
(301) 652-3556
<www.honesttea.com>

Net Impact
(formerly Students for Responsible Business)
609 Mission Street
Third Floor
San Francisco, CA 94105
(415) 778-8366
<www.net-impact.org>

Newman's Own
246 Post Road East
Westport, CT 06880
<www.newmansown.com>

Stonyfield Farm
Ten Burton Drive
Londonderry, NH 03053
(603) 437-5050

The Timberland Company
200 Domain Drive
Stratham, NH 03885
<www.timberland.com>

You & Company
27 Draper Road
Dover, MA 02030-1611
<www.you-company.com>

About the Author

Stephanie Lowell is an Associate at McKinsey & Company, Inc. She has done work in the health care, retail/consumer, government, and nonprofit sectors, including pro bono work for the United Way of Massachusetts Bay, the Boys and Girls Clubs of Boston, and multiple educational institutions. She has a Masters in Business Administration and a Masters in Public Administration, both from Harvard University, and is closely involved with the Harvard Business School Initiative on Social Enterprise.

Lowell's other nonprofit experience includes internships with both Project Hope and Success By 6 (a program of the United Way of Massachusetts Bay). She has also worked with Work/Family Directions, Inc., focusing on child care initiatives. Lowell currently serves on several nonprofit boards, including the Child Care Capital Investment Fund, where she is Assistant Treasurer, and the Steering Committee of the United Way Young Leaders Society.